Praise for

SALES SUCKS...BUT IT DOESN'T HAVE TO

"Mike and Gregg have done a masterful job of weaving stories of their past and present careers into sales tutorials on leadership, character, and trust. This is a must-read, not just by sales professionals, but by anyone in business who wants more."

—**MARK VOGEL**, COO, Bullet EV Charging
and Bullet Solar Solutions

"*Sales Sucks* is an honest and entertaining approach to how to think about sales. It's like reading a great story and taking a sales masterclass all wrapped up in one book—great for both the sales reps and the sales leaders who are trying to make the right transformative move for their teams."

—**STACY ADAMS**, Vice President of Operations, In-Telecom

"I have had the pleasure to work closely with Mike and Gregg to help bring our organization to over a billion dollars in sales. I know firsthand the power of a customized sales tool to enable sales and empower salespeople to close deals with facts. The proven method in this book will show your team how to steer the customer down a path of engagement and turn the sales call into an experience."

—**JERRY CARPENTER**, CRO, Solar Powur ON

"*Sales Sucks* isn't just another sales book. It's your transformation guide. Get ready to ditch the outdated and embrace a proven approach that will skyrocket your sales conversations."

—**JUSTIN BEAM**, Founder, PerformanceiQ

"Keen insights throughout. In *Sales Sucks*, Mike and Gregg have shared years of learnings from their enormous, well earned success. This is a valuable read for any business leader, and a must-read for leaders wanting to grow their business."

—**MARC LEE**, former CEO, Sun Solar

SALES SUCKS

SUCKS

(...BUT IT DOESN'T HAVE TO)

TRANSFORM NEW REPS INTO TOP PERFORMERS

AND SCALE YOUR SALES ORG

FROM MILLIONS TO BILLIONS

MIKE LATCH
AND
GREGG MURPHY

WINDERMERE
PRESS

SALES SUCKS...BUT IT DOESN'T HAVE TO
Transform New Reps into Top Performers and
Scale Your Sales Org from Millions to Billions
First Edition

ISBN		
	978-1-962341-57-8	*Hardcover*
	978-1-962341-56-1	*Paperback*
	978-1-962341-59-2	*Ebook*
	978-1-962341-58-5	*Audiobook*

CONTENTS

FOREWORD

For those of us who have walked the road of scaling a business, growth and challenge often feel like two sides of the same coin. Sometimes it feels like it's a lot more challenge than it is growth—and when it does, you can only hope to have a guidebook like the one you're about to read to help you conquer it.

When our company Sunpro first started, we were a small, ambitious team with a big vision, but only a rudimentary sales process. Like many companies, we'd developed a bare-bones system that involved simple booklets with key product information. Sales reps carried these booklets around in their trunks, flipping through pages with customers during presentations.

Every salesperson had their own "interpretation" of what was important, and it was creating a fractured customer experience; we weren't projecting a unified message, plain and simple, and our sales numbers reflected it. I remember thinking at the time: There has to be a better way.

We needed a cohesive, streamlined system that provided consistency and empowered our sales team with the right tools. The only problem? It didn't exist.

Then I was introduced to Mike Latch, and in that first meeting, I could hardly imagine the transformative impact he would have on our company. Mike's software solution offered exactly what we needed—a customizable, interactive digital format that let customers participate in designing their solar systems. The solution also consolidated all our products into a single, seamless presentation, allowing us to present complex data, options, and pricing in a way that made sense to our customers. It solved the challenge of our disjointed pitches and provided a consistent, comprehensive customer experience.

There was plenty of skepticism within the team when we rolled out the software, but it didn't take long for them to see its value. Over time, Mike's software, along with Gregg Murphy's revolutionary sales process for consultative sales, transformed our operations in ways I couldn't have foreseen. We could now expand into new markets rapidly, setting up new offices and training teams in weeks instead of months. One of the greatest strengths of the software was its ability to make even a brand-new salesperson look like an expert; suddenly, our mid-level sales team saw their closing rates improve drastically, which ultimately had a bigger impact on our bottom line than our top-tier performers alone could have achieved.

Over the years since, I've had the opportunity to consult with other companies in the B2C sector, and I'm frequently struck by how many are still struggling with the same issues we faced early on. Many businesses operate without a clear, standardized sales process, and watching these companies try to make it work reminds me of our early days at Sunpro, before Mike and Gregg transformed our sales org. Most CEOs simply don't understand the power that a unified, dynamic sales system can offer.

This book is for those sales leaders who are ready to take their sales operations to the next level. It outlines a methodology for creating a high-quality, efficient process that can elevate an entire sales team's performance, not just the top 10 or 20 percent. A good process, coupled with the right tools, can turn your mid-tier performers into top sellers, helping you grow faster, reduce training time, and maximize revenue without constantly having to reinvent the wheel. I'd encourage you to keep an open mind as you read this book. There's a chance that the ideas in here will challenge the way you think about sales—but if you're willing to make that leap, as we did, the rewards will be well worth it.

Marc Jones, founder, Sunpro Solar

INTRODUCTION

SALES SUCKS...
BUT IT DOESN'T HAVE TO

If you're a CEO or sales leader who saw the title of this book and thought to yourself, *"Damn straight*, sales sucks," then you're in the right place.

And you're not alone.

One of the things we hear all the time from CEOs, sales managers, and org leaders who are responsible for growing their consultative sales teams is that sales *sucks*. We also hear it from salespeople themselves. So many of them are struggling, frustrated, and have a negative view of the role. They feel pushy. They feel disliked. They often feel underprepared and somehow, at the same time, they feel like the customer just can't keep up.

Getting sales = awesome. Doing sales = often a total drag.

Speaking of the customer, they're yet another group that would totally, wholeheartedly agree with the conjecture that *sales sucks*. The general public has a deep disdain for selling because they view sales reps as conniving and pushy, trying to manipulate prospects rather than identifying and meeting their needs. There's some truth to this perception, especially with big-ticket items, but it's not entirely the fault of the reps. That's just how they've been trained to make sales.

In smaller sales teams, or at companies just starting out, many sales reps lack a clear and consistent sales process. Instead, they've picked up a few tactics here and there piecemeal from sales managers that are geared toward coercing or manipulating customers to make a sale. They push and prod relentlessly because they've been led to believe that's how sales are made. For customers, the whole experience sucks, and they wind up feeling irritated instead of engaged.

It doesn't matter how awesome a product or service is—if the sales reps come across as inauthentic and deceptive, the product and even the company as a whole take a hit. As a result, sales managers have a hard time hitting their sales numbers. Customer satisfaction rates are lower than they should be. And great companies with amazing products are getting less of the market than they could (or should).

So, yes. Sales sucks.

But it doesn't have to.

You can have sales teams that win more of their opportunities and level up seemingly overnight—*without* hiring different people or dumping more money into training.

We wrote this book to share three things with you:

A proven sales process that has helped sales teams go from treading water to explosive growth.

A step-by-step guide to creating the tools and technology that will turn even mediocre sales reps into superstars.

A framework for introducing this new process and tech to your entire organization so that your teams can break out and run.

We didn't always have these things nailed down, though. So how the hell did we find ourselves writing a book?

GREGG: THE PROCESS GUY

When Mike first came to the solar business, let's just say I had my doubts about him.

Mike didn't come from a sales background, but rather a science and engineering background. He seemed to have the personality of a cyborg. On our initial phone call, he was dry and flat, without any of the charisma I'd expect from a good sales rep. I only met with him at the insistence of the company's CEO, and it took about three minutes for me to come to the conclusion: *This guy will never make it in sales.*

Now, to be fair to Mike, he didn't realize I was going to be so closely scrutinizing his personality on that brief phone call, so he was simply trying to be polite and professional. He assumed he was being offered a job. He was pretty shocked when he was told there was no opening for him.

After that abrupt rejection, most people would never have come back, but Mike isn't most people. The next day, he sent me a lengthy email in which he laid out his case (in a sense, a sales presentation about his own suitability for the position). Mike may have lacked a lot in the personality department, but he'd shown me one of the key traits of a successful salesperson: he wouldn't stop at "no," and his email demonstrated that he was smart, determined, and willing to fight for what he thought was right. So, against every inner voice telling me that training this guy as a salesman was going to be like pushing rocks uphill, I decided to give him a chance.

Turns out that if you take a scientific mind (Mike's) and a rigorously proven sales process (mine) and you put them together, personality isn't that big a piece of the equation. Mike memorized my sales process verbatim and immediately began applying it in the field.

Within a few weeks, Mike came back with a handful of lucrative contracts. When our astonished CEO asked Mike how he'd closed so many deals so quickly, he said, "I'm just doing exactly what Gregg told me to do!"

I'll admit, I was astonished as well. Somehow, the guy who had bored me to tears during our first conversation had become a sales superstar within a matter of weeks. What the hell was his secret?

Simple: Mike had a knack for improvisation that turned around more objections than even the senior reps were usually capable of. It turns out that robot brain of his had been able to memorize so much about the product that every time a conversation with a customer veered off course, he knew exactly how to problem-solve and get things moving in the right direction again. On top of that, Mike had done exactly what he told our CEO: simply what I had taught him. He'd been given a good sales process with a great script that communicated the value of the product, and he shared it *exactly as written* with prospective clients. No tricks, no coercion, no winging it, and no shady tactics. He did his thing, listened to customers, offered solutions to objections, and helped lead them to a decision they felt good about. That enabled him to perform at the top, when it took other reps years to perform at the same level.

That's the power of a good consultative sales process. If you can take a guy as seemingly ill-suited to sales as my co-author and turn him into a top sales rep in a matter of weeks, you know your process works.

We're going to teach you this process in the chapters to come, but there's more to the story—you're also going to learn how to leverage technology to make that process soar.

MIKE: THE TECHNICAL GUY

I know Gregg hates that I instantly crushed at sales when he thought I'd crash and burn. What can I say—I like subverting expectations.

I came into sales with the mindset of this book's title: sales *sucks*. My father was an engineer, his father was an engineer, and my mother's father was an engineer. You can see how I grew up thinking that sales and marketing were unnecessary; that well-engineered products sold themselves. My entire concept of sales was the way my parents would get annoyed at the slimy inauthenticity of car salesmen. So, years later, when I started my own career in R&D at a defense contractor and the other engineers mentioned that I would be good in sales, I took it as an insult! It took becoming a salesperson myself and seeing happy customers and success with Gregg's effective and ethical sales process to change my mind.

When I became Gregg's top sales rep, it wasn't because I was doing anything especially innovative. Far from it; I was doing exactly what I was told. I also happen to have an analytical brain that I've been told resembles software—hence Gregg's initial skepticism about my fitness for a sales role. I like to problem-solve. When I was on sales calls, I'd address edge case situations more often than other new reps who were out of their element whenever a customer threw a wrench in their scripted conversation. This naturally led to a higher close rate *and* higher customer satisfaction, which led to more one-call closes.

But while I was working Gregg's script and bringing in sales, my technical background was internally screaming at the mess of sales enablement software I and the rest of the sales team I was a part of were using. I've never been a guy who cared all that much about being liked, so I spent a fair amount of time emailing our vendors and partners pointing out ways their software could be better. That, plus becoming the company's top rep by every metric they had within three months, caused the President to ask if I would take over a critical endeavor at the company: building their own sales enablement application in line with their vision of expanding their company into a solar franchise that spanned the country.

Fast forward a few years later, and I was running a software development company in San Diego trying to answer those questions. The CEO of Sunpro, a guy named Marc Jones, came knocking, wanting a sales tool and he only knew that he wasn't crazy about what their team was currently using and that nothing else in the market really resonated with him. I didn't know it at the time, but Marc has great intuition for what experiences will be deemed to be good and solid by both consumers and business people alike. This is why he was never happy with any of the off-the-shelf sales enablement applications he'd seen.

When I met Marc, I had a vision for how the world of sales (later, I would learn what I really understood well about sales was in the area of consultative sales and value selling) could be better through technology, but I didn't then know enough about raising money, SaaS profit margin requirements, and the multitude of other skills I've since picked up. What I did have was an application that was custom built to facilitate an extremely engaging and interactive sales appointment. This software that would allow other sales reps to have the kind of customer agency maximizing, design-from-scratch-while-the-customer-watches-me-do-it experiences that allowed me to be an elite seller very quickly.

When I demonstrated what we had planned to go to market with to Sunpro, they had recently grown operations out of their home state of Louisiana and into Texas—and with that scaling came problems. Marc was seeing a rapid decline in the consistency of how his sales team was performing as more territories and reps were added to his business. He hired my team to continue developing our app and gave me carte blanche to design it as I saw fit. (I love when people do that.) When it was time, I flew out to the pilot territory to personally train their sales team on the app. I also spent a week going on sales ride-alongs with the sales manager. Our software was untested, and Sunpro had taken a big risk on us.

It paid off. The following month, sales increased by an insane 37 percent in the pilot territory.

Even their "C" reps, people who could barely close a sale to save their lives, were suddenly closing left and right.

As Sunpro rolled out the app in territory after territory, the success just skyrocketed. This was a company with no outside capital, operating in a crazy competitive industry where sales reps deal with tons of restrictions—and using the process and technology you'll learn in this book, they managed to grow from $45 million in annual sales to a $1 billion run rate in four years. *Bootstrapped*.

They were also able to bring in an ever-increasing flow of new sales reps—doubling the number of reps every year—and train them up so quickly that they were out in the field closing sales and performing at a high level within just a couple of weeks.

It came as no surprise that the company wanted more—specifically, Sunpro wanted the entire org to have a "badass" sales presentation in their back pocket, and asked if our team could take that on.

"Sure," I replied, "But it'll cost me time and focus on all the product dev I'm doing for you. Instead, I've got the guy you should call." I gave him Gregg's number.

Gregg's process, my software—that's the secret weapon we decided someone needed to write a book on. (We didn't initially realize that someone needed to be us, but eventually, we got there.

IT'S NOT A PEOPLE PROBLEM

Okay, *sometimes* it is.

But what if it didn't have to be?

What if you could take your C and B players and bring them up to—okay, not A players, maybe, but at the very least B+ players—right away?

Without spending all your time training them? On average, it takes anywhere from eight to eighteen months to create a "veteran" performer out of a new consultative sales rep. What if you could cut that time to a fraction, and get them there almost instantly? *Without* waiting for their sales averages to slowly crawl up as they learn the ropes?

Or, think of it this way: imagine your most seasoned sales rep. The absolute best person you have. They can rattle off every single detail about the product without blinking an eye. Any objection the customer throws at them, they know how to reroute into an opportunity. They can improvise and tell a great story like the best writers in Hollywood.

Because that's really what sales is about: telling a great story. Humans have developed no more effective way of delivering information from one brain to another than through a compelling story. Consider how easy it would be for you, right now and with no preparation, to convey the major plot points of a popular story—whether it be *Romeo and Juliet* or *Top Gun*. It's easy because our human brains have evolved to receive messages, assign importance, and remember information best when it's conveyed in story form.

But your newer sales reps take longer to learn that story and the script that sells it best. They take a while to get comfortable with it no matter what the customer comes back with. They miss opportunities that your A player top rep easily closes on a regular basis, because they can navigate the relevant topics so damn well. Sometimes, it's because they need more experience. Sometimes it's because they're bad at the job. Either way, you find yourself wishing you could just send your A player rep to talk to every single customer.

Well, what if you could? What if you could send your A player to *every sales interaction* along with each one of your less-seasoned reps? What if they could be there with them to fill in the gaps on all those opportunities they're missing? What if you could get just one or two more sales every month from the middle-performing 80% of your sales team?

Across a sales org with dozens or hundreds of reps, that translates into *wild* increases in sales.

Again, this isn't a silver bullet. You're not taking every single sales rep and turning them into a superstar. (That's what defines a superstar: there aren't that many of them.) What you're doing is leveling up your reps who are *not* the superstars. Take a look at this bell curve:

B PLAYERS

C PLAYERS

A PLAYERS

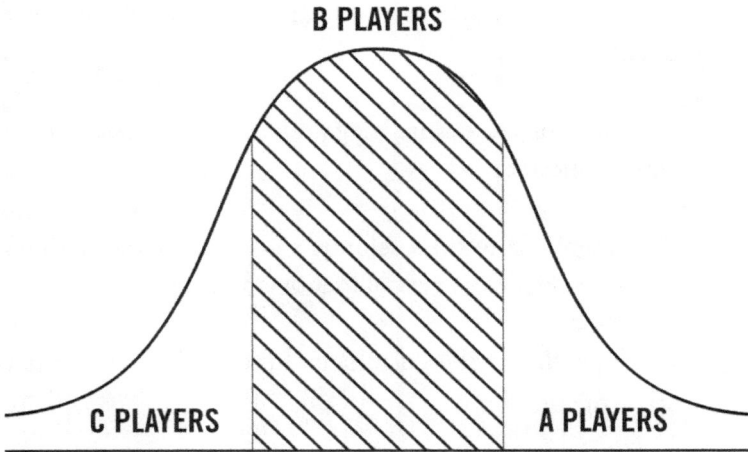

On the right end, you have your A players. Your superstars. All the way at the left end, you have your C players—new reps just finding their footing, or more seasoned reps who might not be right for the role. Then, in the middle shaded area, the vast majority of the curve, you have your B players. If you could shift up the close averages of that entire middle section up a couple of percentage points, the increase in sales would be massive.

That's what this book is going to teach you. More than that, we'll give you a roadmap for developing and implementing the same strategy in your own company.

Our approach to sales sounds deceptively simple:

1. Present information to the customer using a compelling

story arc so it makes sense to them and speaks to their needs.

2. Ask questions to ensure they understand the value being communicated.

3. Try to anticipate the customer's objections and address them in advance as part of that overarching story.

4. Be respectful of the customer's time and preserve their sense of autonomy.

If your product is complicated, expend great effort in training sales reps and leverage customized sales technology to make it simple for the customer to understand. Expend great effort in building tech that preserves more of the customer's sense of autonomy throughout the sales appointment.

At the most basic level, that's it. Now, that last bullet point is *way* harder than it probably sounds, but we'll spend a few chapters talking you through it. Before we do that, let us be clear, you will be in the best position to leverage technology in the way we teach if you understand the early chapters on script creation and the sales process. When you can train your salespeople to follow a story-driven consultative sales process consistently out in the field, you'll get a much higher level of performance across the board. And that will position you well to incorporate a customized sales tool.

With an effective script *and* a good sales tool, you will make your sales team far more responsive and get customers to make buying decisions much faster, far more often, and with a much higher degree of after-sale satisfaction than you ever have before. We've seen this firsthand. It's hard to overstate just how much of an impact these things will make on your outcomes.

Of course, creating technology tools requires a rare skill set, but we're going to show you how to do it. In the following chapters, you'll get step-by-step guidance for creating an effective process, training your team, and designing tech tools tailored to your product and target audience.

WHAT IS CONSULTATIVE SALES?

If you haven't worked in consultative sales before, here's a quick rundown. Consultative sales describes the sales process for a particular type of product or service. This product or service has the following traits:

- It's complex and configurable enough that there isn't one clear "way" it will be sold—rather, the customer's unique needs define what flavor they'll end up with, so the sales rep needs to be able to help the customer think critically about what their true needs are.

- There are multiple ways the product or service could be leveraged to solve the customer's true needs, so it needs to be customized based on a strategy that gets them the biggest amount of their top-priority solutions.

When a customer buys a pack of gum, it's a transactional sale: you hand them gum, they hand you money. But when a customer buys a solar energy system for their house, the sheer volume of variables that need to be considered and matched up with the right options requires a lot of knowledge and a lot of problem-solving. It also requires next-level listening skills; the customer doesn't always know what they actually want, need, or even have the ability to get, so the consultative sales rep needs to listen for what's not being said and read between the lines a fair amount. The customer doesn't know what they don't know. It's up to the sales rep to help them navigate the web of variables that will lead them to a decision.

Consultative sales teams currently do this with lengthy, complex sales scripts that get the job done *if* the customer doesn't raise an objection that irrevocably derails the script. Veteran sales reps have built a reference library of knowledge about each of these objections and can skillfully navigate them—but it takes an immense amount of time to get a new sales rep to that level.

Or, at least, it *did*. In this book, you're going to learn how to shorten that time from years or months to *days*.

LET'S GO

What you've read here is certainly a *simplified* version of our story, and the journey from meeting each other to writing this book came with a lot more speedbumps than you need us to exhaustively detail. (Maybe someday when we write our autobiographies—but that's not this book.)

Sunpro is one of many examples you'll read about in this book, and pretty soon your own company, if you take what's in these pages to heart, will join them on their sales success rocketship.

Or maybe things are going well for you right now. Your team is rocking sales, your script seems fine, and your tech is good enough. Well, here's a bit of a wake-up call: your good fortune might change next quarter. A good sales process should be a living thing. What was optimal yesterday may not be optimal tomorrow (or today, for that matter). You have to be willing to adapt and change along the way—the same way your A player sales reps do in every customer interaction. And if you don't have the right tech in place to enable your B and C players to successfully navigate the complex web of product knowledge, customer objections, and sophisticated value proposition during the entirety of each and every sales appointment, you're leaving money on the table, plain and simple.

So no matter how well (or not so well) your sales team is currently performing, you're going to pick up some new ideas in this book that you can implement *right now* to take your team up a level.

In short: yes, sales sucks. But only if you don't turn the page to Chapter One.

Let's go.

PART

ONE

THE PROCESS

CHAPTER ONE

WHAT'S WRONG WITH SALES?

In most cases, sales reps *mean* well.

They're not trying to be icky. Or pushy. Or annoying,

They just haven't been trained to confidently present their product with openness and humility. Instead, they rely on leading questions that attempt to force customers toward a predetermined end. You know the kinds of questions we're talking about:

"You wouldn't want to spend $45,000 dollars on your utility when I could offer the same service for $35,000, would you? Wouldn't saving $10,000 be best for you and your family?"

"Our baby-safe tires only cost $800. You wouldn't want something bad to happen to your baby, would you? For the cost of seventeen lattes a month, you will keep your baby safe. Isn't your baby's life

worth more than seventeen lattes?"

And so on.

These are bad faith questions. The rep isn't seeking an honest answer or trying to gain clarity about the customer's needs. Instead, they are manipulating the customer to agree with their premise by making it seem like any other response makes the customer look stupid.

"Well, *of course* my baby's life is worth the cost of seventeen lattes! Only a horrible person would say no!"

This is the underlying psychology of the typical sales experience, and it's why people often feel like they need to take a shower afterward. Leading questions take away the customer's autonomy by creating hypothetical situations where the customer can only choose to do what the rep wants.

This creates psychological reluctance on the part of the customer because they feel their freedom and self-determination deteriorating during the process. When you tell someone they *have* to do something, they instantly feel a level of resistance because they are not being allowed to choose. Even if you succeed in getting them to do what you want (in this case, buy your product), they will walk away feeling like they lost a battle with an enemy.

But when there's a good process and a solid script in place—a script peppered with questions and answers to common customer issues that help both customer and sales rep come to the same conclusion together—then the goal ceases to be "my way or the highway." Instead of trying to get a yes at all costs (even if the cost is the customer's impression of you and your company), you optimize the chances that a customer will reach a decision that they are happy with.

And if you both agree that buying is *not* the right decision, then you can shake hands, and the customer will go on their merry way with *no hard feelings*. That's always preferable to pushing them into a buying decision that feels wrong—it's certainly better for the reputation of your sales reps, product, and company.

IT'S TIME TO STOP!

The best salespeople are not trying to defeat the customer by strong-arming them into a sale at any cost. Rather, they are trying to help the customer make a great decision by using a script that presents a lot of useful information, addresses objections, and leads them to that decision in a way they both feel good about. The best reps ask, "Does that make sense?" a lot and listen carefully to the customer's responses so they know if they're doing a good job at explaining the value of the product.

Only with real clarity can the customer make a decision that they feel good about, and only with a good process and script can the customer achieve real clarity on a large percentage of sales calls.

Of course, the best sales process in the world does you no good if your reps don't follow it consistently. If they're out in the field winging it, saying all kinds of things, and having a heck of a good time listening to themselves talk—that's not a sales process, that's chaos, and customers won't consistently engage. It is much easier to grow sales with consistent performance from your sales team. This is why a good salesperson at a company that *wants to grow fast* is someone who is *trainable* and *coachable,* not just someone with swagger and a big personality. It is much more difficult to scale sales, and the sales team, if your only successful sales people sell through charisma or other hard to teach skills.

At the same time, your old sales process might have been decent at one time, but the world has changed. Your customers have access to the internet, so they have more information at their fingertips. They are savvier and more cynical about your old sales techniques, so they respond with greater hostility to anything they perceive as deceptive or coercive.

The idea that we have to coerce and connive in order to land a customer is an outdated methodology. Customers hate it, and a lot of sales reps these days hate it, too. Most of your reps, especially the younger generations, don't enjoy dragging customers kicking and screaming over to their way of thinking. They would rather make an impact and feel good about the work they're doing in the world. And that's part of the reason why turnover among sales reps is so high.

Now, you might be tempted to point to one of your top performers and argue, "If my methodology is outdated, then why is my top sales rep killing it out in the field? Shouldn't my other reps emulate this guy?"

And we would say, some of those high-performing reps are incredibly charismatic and they can coast on their natural charm. You can't look at them as proof that your process is working because *they're probably not following your process.*

You don't necessarily need to stack your team with big personalities. In fact, it's harder to scale a team if you're only looking for big personalities, because there simply aren't as many super smart, charismatic people out there who can charm, thrust, and parry their way through complicated consultative sales.

You will get much better performance across the board if you train reps to stick to your process than if you try to hire a bunch of charismatic charmers—but only if your process is highly effective.

PULL THE LEVER

Look, every sales rep has the same goal. They're all trying to get to the "yes" and walk away with the sale—plain and simple. However, in order to get to the *yes*, you also have to embrace the *no*. In other words, you have to empower your salespeople to help customers make decisions that they feel good about. Period.

Chances are, since you're reading this book, you know things could be better. Maybe your current process is pushy and forceful, but "pushy" doesn't create a safe environment for a customer to make a confident decision, and it doesn't create a high quality sales experience. Nor does it generally lead to optimal results. It might work at first, but at some point, the negative customer consequences of pushy sales create tremendous headwinds due to bad reviews, cancellations, skyrocketing customer support costs, and so on.

Fortunately there is one lever you can pull that will make a massive difference, and that's *process*: how you and your sales reps relate to customers and help them make a decision. A sales manager, and the script they create, lays the foundation for success or failure out in the field. And what does success look like? A sale, a happy customer, and profit.

To get all three, we recommend delivering the relevant information with a high-quality story that any member of your team can share in the same way every time. When that happens, a lot of the "suckiness" will disappear. Because when you have a high-quality process that tells a compelling story, your salespeople won't be out there asking leading questions; they will be providing valuable information. They won't be prompting customers to give them the right answer; they will bring them to clarity. They won't waste people's time; they will have authentic (maybe even enjoyable) interactions.

THE HAPPY PATH

Of course, no salesperson can know everything. Even if they are trained to deliver an effective, empathetic, and ethical explanation of the value proposition of a product, there are going to be things they don't know, so there are bound to be customer questions that they simply can't answer on the spot. If your process and technology don't address this, then the new sales rep will be forced to think on their feet, and often they're going to deliver a poor quality answer.

But how in the world can you train your sales reps to address every possible question that customers might have? How can you weave answers to every possible objection into the script? Quite frankly, you can't, not if you want to respect the customer's time, so here's how we handle it:

Generally, we think about the sales process in terms of the Happy Path, primary objections, and secondary objections. The Happy Path is a script that explains the things a customer needs to know and answers the questions customers generally need answered in order to make a buying decision they'll be happy with. It doesn't attempt to address every possible objection or answer every possible question, because there's usually no need.

You know you are in the right ballpark for a Happy Path sales process if it alone will deliver about half of your sales. That is, on about half of the sales appointments, the sales rep can simply walk the customer down the Happy Path, and the customer will make a decision at the end that they feel good about. Therefore, the Happy Path is the script that every rep is going to deliver every time, and it is crafted to find the right balance between thoroughness and the customer's time (and how long a person can pay attention to a sales rep).

However, you also have to train your sales team to handle the most common questions (i.e. primary objections), which tend to come up the other half of the time. The rep doesn't need to bring these answers up in advance—only if the customer asks a question. Remember, you're trying to respect the customer's time and autonomy. That's why you stick to the Happy Path unless an objection is raised by the customer.

Many scripts try to overcome every objection in one shot, but this often creates objections in the customer's mind that they didn't have before. It adds confusion, and a confused mind can't make a decision with as much clarity and confidence.

Secondary objections are the questions customers rarely ask and, in some cases, questions no rep can anticipate. In fact, they may be so rare that you don't have training material on dealing with them. In that case, your reps can address them by saying something like, "That's a great question. I've never been asked that before. You have put a lot of thought into this. You are one of the most informed customers I've met. I don't know the answer right now, but I'm going to get it for you. I'm sorry to use up your time and not have that answer at my fingertips."

By complimenting them on their question, you make the customer feel smart. You embrace the relationship, and trust is formed. And the more comfortable they feel asking questions, the more they will drop their guard. In this way, you can maintain the truth and preserve the authenticity of the interaction, even if the rep doesn't have a ready answer.

We'll delve into this approach more deeply in the next chapter, but we wanted to introduce the concept now. To summarize, you're creating a Happy Path script that sales reps will use every time and then additional scripts for primary objections that they can turn to if the customer asks common questions.

What you *never* want your reps to do is fake it. Trying to fake answers is one of the primary contributing factors to a good sales rep's performance degrading over time. We've all seen it. A rep gets lazy, they start overtalking, coming up with off-the-cuff answers, getting lost in tangents, and they forget what made them good to begin with.

Remember, the goal of the sales process you're going to create is to build trust and communicate value clearly so customers can make an honest, informed decision. There's no need to fake anything.

YOUR TECHNOLOGY SUCKS

Sometimes, your sales process isn't the problem. It's the sales technology your reps are using. Tech that is supposed to make the process go more smoothly can instead become a pain in the ass. Bouncing back and forth between the conversation and various sales tools (e.g., PowerPoint presentation, spreadsheets, visual configuration software, sales enablement software, spec sheets, etc.) might make the whole sales pitch feel clunky, or the tech might not be especially user friendly.

We found that off-the-shelf software could not deliver the sales performance that our internally developed technology could, because of our own requirements and standards associated with what is a good enough experience between the sales rep and client. Most off-the-shelf software doesn't facilitate the natural flow of a sales pitch, doesn't encourage design input and decisions by the end customer, isn't tailored nearly enough to your company and specific market, and what makes you stand out against your competitors, and using the tech feels like forcing square pegs into round holes. It's far from optimal. Gregg and Mike lead Sales and Tech, respectively, at two prior companies. At both we found that we were able to grow 3X compared with our competitors (we could consistently deliver around 100% CAGR growth all the way up to $1B+ in sales with no outside capital while competitors also growing off their own profits were typically maxing out around 30% CAGR (unless they were very small companies)).

If your sales technology doesn't help generate revenue similarly, then expect better! If it's not helping sales reps when they're in front of a customer, then challenge whoever on your team is bringing you this tool to come up with something better.

So much of the tech out there today is lacking big time. You need better tech, and if you're big enough that the fixed costs of building your own great tools makes sense, then you should seriously consider investing in customized sales tech that will give you a competitive edge. In fact, we're going to walk you through the process of creating it in later chapters. Customized software isn't cheap, and it may not make ROI sense for a smaller company, but if you're a bigger company, then it's absolutely worth a look. The growth we experienced would have been impossible without the technology we had to build ourselves.

Gregg was the first to explain to Mike that a sales rep's job isn't just about pushing a product—it's about helping the customer make an informed decision that's truly in their best interest. When you're selling a complex, customizable product like a home energy system with solar panels, batteries, and energy efficiency solutions, it's not always clear how to make sure the homeowner fully understands their options. Most sales reps typically show up with a pre-designed solution, then explain why it's the right fit for the customer. But if they uncover new information during the sales meeting that makes the original proposal no longer the best option, they face two choices. The first is to downplay the issue and try to keep the customer focused on the original solution. The second is to revise the design on the spot or offer to reschedule the meeting so they can come up with a new solution. Clearly, the first option isn't ideal for the customer or the business in the long run.

And that's where Mike found a huge opportunity for growth—by setting higher expectations for both the sales and tech teams when it comes to enabling sales. There's a unique dynamic between the sales and tech leaders that can unlock real potential in the sales team.

The sales leadership should expect the following during every sales appointment:

1. Only one application should be used, whether it's on a tablet or laptop, and it should be the focal point throughout the meeting for both the rep and the customer.

2. Every topic and decision should be supported and guided by the application.

3. There should be no off-topic information—nothing on the screen that could confuse the customer or steer the conversation off track.

4. Over time, any features in the application that require explaining or "doing ahead of time" should be minimized. Instead, the experience should shift toward "designing from scratch," where the customer is making decisions along the way, guided by the rep, until they arrive at a solution that suits their needs.

On the tech side, the leadership should expect this:

1. They should be an active partner in developing and refining the sales methodology used in appointments.

2. Their teams working on sales enablement tools should be attending sales appointments.

3. Their teams should be experts on the sales process, including knowing the sales scripts inside and out.

The relationship between the sales and tech leaders is absolutely critical. There needs to be a high level of trust and collaboration between them. This trust isn't built overnight—it's earned through repeated help and support, where neither side looks for someone to blame when things go wrong, but instead asks, "What can I do to prevent this from happening again?" Tech leaders and their teams, working on sales enablement tools, should feel like an unofficial part of the sales team. Likewise, sales leaders and their teams should feel like an unofficial part of the tech team.

One of the biggest reasons Sunpro was able to scale so quickly—growing from a $45M in sales to a $1B+ run rate in less than four years—was the special influence sales had with tech. This was made possible by Marc, our CEO and Founder, who fostered a culture where tech was allowed to play an active, supportive role in sales, and vice versa. That collaboration was key to unlocking the company's full potential.

Like we mentioned in the Introduction, skepticism from sales reps was something we dealt with early on. Like with Jerry Carpenter, a former sales exec with experience at SolarCity and Tesla, who Mike connected with Gregg. Jerry had come up through Yellow Pages, where he received some of the best sales training you could ask for. At Yellow Pages, they were masters at helping businesses secure advertising budgets, and Jerry was one of their top reps. He brought that same level of professionalism and know-how to the solar industry, quickly climbing the ranks at SolarCity.

When Gregg first hired Jerry at Sunpro, Jerry wasn't sure what to expect. He'd seen plenty of companies where the sales process was weak, and he assumed Sunpro would be just another one of those. His first sales ride-along with one of our reps didn't exactly impress him, either; he thought the rep was average at best.

But then he saw the software.

The rep walked through our sales enablement application, and Jerry was blown away by how effective and simple it made the entire process. The app, combined with our sales scripts, was a game-changer. Jerry went from being skeptical to becoming a huge believer in our sales call process. He quickly realized that the tools we had in place were different from anything he had seen before, and he dove in headfirst.

Over time, Jerry became a key player in helping Gregg grow the sales team, eventually becoming his right-hand man.

CONFRONTING A COMPETITIVE LANDSCAPE

At Sunpro, the sales leadership team was represented by Gregg (the CRO), Jerry (Gregg's number two), and Shaan Rahi, Jerry's most trusted subordinate. At the time, Shaan was already managing a sales team of hundreds, and he was known as one of the most dependable managers in the company. When Shaan was sent to underperforming territories, he quickly figured out the problem every single time: the reps weren't following the sales call process.

Shaan, being highly competitive with a background in collegiate sports, saw the situation much like a coach watching players miss key plays. In sports, when a team doesn't perform, it often comes down to the players not executing the plays correctly. And in sales, the same concept applied—if performance was lacking, it was usually because the reps weren't "running the play."

This idea stuck, and Shaan coined the term "run the play," which quickly became a mantra for the entire team. It was a simple, clear way to remind everyone what was expected of them: *follow the process.*

When you're at your best, the competition is more likely to begin emulating your process. They copy you, and now they're giving your sales reps a run for their money. Well, guess what? That's good news. It indicates that you're lifting up and elevating the entire industry. That's what we all want, isn't it? It just means you always have to be out front. You have to be on the leading edge. And in order to do that, you have to have great processes and tools that can adapt to changing conditions.

If you're freaking out because you used to have exclusivity but then you lost it, it's time for a reality check: being successful because of a monopoly doesn't guarantee that your company delivers a high-quality sales experience to customers. When exclusivity goes away, that's when you really learn how to sell. Because if the competition offers a similar product, especially if yours is at a higher price point, then you'd better be able to show customers why you're better. We say *show*, because you can't simply *tell*.

Now, that doesn't mean you have to be able to prove you're better than your competition beyond a shadow of a doubt or provide enough mathematical proof that your superiority is irrefutable. You're simply saying, "Look, we believe we're a great company with an excellent product at a reasonable price point," then providing enough evidence that the customer will understand your reasoning and see the logic in your claim.

That evidence can take the form of third-party referrals, reviews, your standing in the community, your NPS or something else, as long as it makes your claim of being a superior company with a superior product seem reasonable.

If your company *isn't* the best, then you should either be trying to make it better, or you should consider going somewhere else. You need to believe in your company and your product if your sales reps are going to create authentic conversations with customers and share the value you deliver. If you're a sales manager and you feel hamstrung by leadership and unable to make your team any better than it is, perhaps it's time to head for the exit. You don't want to be forced to stand in front of your sales team and lie to them—telling them the company, product or service is amazing, when they're not.

In order to stay competitive, the sales call plan must constantly change. Here are the three stages of a process to continually improve the sales call plan:

When you have high convergence between tech and sales, your company can break down the steps above into the following:

1. Create or modify the sales call plan:

   a. Visual configuration

   b. Topics, scripts and pitching user experiences

   c. Alignment with business objectives

   d. Script and pitch analysis

   e. Problem-solution chaining in scripts and pitches

   f. Product offering

    g.   Client agency maximization ("design from scratch user experiences")

    h.   Respect maximization (ensuring absence of leading questions)

2. Ensure the sales call plan is executed properly during sales calls:

    a.   Ride-alongs (physical or generative AI based captures)

    b.   Action plan generation based on deviation from Standards measured on sales appointments, with follow up

3. Measure sales call effectiveness:

    a.   Do the following areas of the standards need to change based on new offerings, competition, or other external factors?

    b.   Scripts

    c.   User experiences

    d.   Training programs

BORING BUT PREDICTABLE

People think of sales as an art form. They think, "Either you have it or you don't. You can either sell ice in a snowstorm or you can't." Many sales managers think this way, usually because they themselves were the kinds of salespeople who crushed it in some non-repeatable way using their own natural swagger.

They now assume that talent and swagger are the only markers of a good salesperson, which means they have a very small percentage of the population to pull from. That makes it harder to scale and harder to talk about why they succeed, because the truth is it's all very chaotic. It's the luck of the draw.

In reality, the best sales experience for your customers is more of a science than an artform. By leveraging the concepts in this book, your company will be able to get higher performance from a significantly larger cross-section of the population, because far more people will be available for you to hire and train to a competent level.

Sales should be boring enough that you can explain exactly how you're going to sell, and everyone should get it. You should be able to get your team up to speed in days with the right tech, rather than months or quarters, and you should be able to tell anyone who wants in on the process (other departments, the

CEO, etc.) exactly what's being said in the customer's "living room" (whether it's in person or on a video call) and how objections are handled.

When you make the sales experience a repeatable process, you can draw from a lot of different bodies of knowledge (e.g., manufacturing, process engineering) to optimize it.

Mike was the one who understood early on the role that technology could play in optimizing the sales experience. It was his vision to maximize customer agency using customized sales technology that would support the sales process, enable reps to demonstrate value with significantly fewer words and far fewer mistakes, and respond to even the most difficult customer questions on the fly than they otherwise could.

But in order for this to work, you have to make sure the tech and script are aligned. Imagine if your company could achieve high ROI with sales enablement tech that guided reps through presenting, configuring, pricing, and quoting all in one application.

The fact is, sales doesn't have to suck! In the following chapters, we're going to explore how you can create a gold standard sales process with a story-driven script that helps reps and customers reach an authentic decision point that they both feel good about.

Then we'll look at how you train reps to this standard so they perform consistently out in the field. Finally, we'll explore how you can design and implement custom software that enables your reps to deliver the story far more effectively and proactively address objections on the fly, maximizing customer autonomy every time. Along the way, we'll share examples from our own experience so you can see how all of this looks in action.

We say this with confidence: **a good script-based consultative sales process combined with customized sales tech creates a rocketship to growth!** You could be achieving *so much more* than you ever thought possible, and we hope you catch the vision in the following chapters.

CHAPTER TWO

TELL A GOOD STORY

If you're selling candy bars from a kiosk in the local shopping mall (i.e., transactional sales), you don't need a thirty-minute sales script to help a customer to make a buying decision. However, highly configurable products often demand *consultative* (as opposed to transactional) sales processes, and in that case, creating a compelling sales script is of paramount importance.

In this chapter, we're going to delve into the process of developing a sales script. This process is particularly well-suited for companies that already have product/market fit. Just to clarify, when we talk about your "sales script," we're actually referring to what would more accurately be called a *sales appointment method,* consisting of all the scripts, questions, and experiences the sales rep is expected to execute during the sales call.

You will create a primary default sales script along with individual scripts for dealing with specific objections. Additionally, depending on your business, you may also have numerous localized scripts for different areas in which you sell. Your default script is what we call the Happy Path, which, as we explained earlier, is the script that every rep is going to deliver every time. You're also going to create scripts to deal with "primary" objections, which are objections customers bring up in 10 to 50 percent of sales calls. But unless a customer brings up one of these primary objections, the sales rep is going to stick to the Happy Path.

> If your company has a single application designed to handle the entire sales appointment process—and you have control over the app's development—you can set much higher goals for your sales calls. For example, back in 2019, it was standard in the solar industry that if a customer needed a new roof before installing solar, a separate roofing sales rep would need to visit the home. But with our sales enablement application, Sunpro's reps could handle both aspects of the sale. Because of the app, we could set a clear goal for the sales call: "If the customer needs a new roof, sell a roof."

Ultimately, our sales script creation process involves the following steps:

1. Defining the Sales Call Goal

2. Defining the Value Proposition

3. Building the Script

   a. Conveying the Value Proposition

   b. Ensuring everything you need to present is contained in a concise story-driven script (or, at least, a problem/solution structure).

   c. Here's an overview of what that looks like.

Before you start creating your script, you have to define the goal of a sales rep's first sales meeting. For a complex or expensive product, it may be unrealistic to expect a customer to sign a contract by the end of the first meeting, in which case your sales reps might need to work toward a more achievable objective. For example, maybe the goal of the first sales meeting is to instill belief in the client regarding the profitability of your solution so they will inquire about the next steps to becoming a client.

With your goal in mind, you can begin meticulously dissecting the sales process, identifying key touchpoints and potential questions that prospective customers might ask. First, map out the order of events, carefully considering the dynamics that will help a customer make an informed buying decision.

Craft the script to unfold like a narrative that tells an overarching story about your value proposition. This ensures a smooth transition from one concept to the next.

The real science lies in presenting information in a way that not only answers current questions but also preempts and addresses the next set of concerns. However, it is vitally important to recognize the limits of the human attention span. You have to set a reasonable threshold for your script's duration, because at some point, customers are going to get bored or frustrated that you're still talking.

The challenge, of course, lies in distilling a vast wealth of information into a concise, engaging narrative that will hold a customer's attention and propel them towards a decision point.

For that reason, assembling a good script is usually an iterative process that involves trial and error, role-playing, and constant refinement. Your team should evaluate each section and gauge its potential impact on the customer's decision-making process. Only the most essential and impactful elements should find a place in the script. Leave no room for fluff or extraneous details. Respect the customer's time!

If your organization uses an in-house application for managing the entire sales appointment process, and you control its development, then building effective scripts will involve close collaboration with the sales technology enablement team. This partnership will help create high-performing scripts and appointment experiences that more of your sales team can execute effectively with the aid of enablement tech.

Take the example of adjusting a sales goal to also pitch a new roof installation if necessary. Here, tech and sales worked together to design a simple user experience in the software, along with an easy-to-follow script that can be used if a customer needs a new roof before installing solar panels.

Another advantage of controlling your own tech is the ability to create "design-from-scratch" scenarios that even mid-level reps can handle. This means developing scripts for situations once thought manageable only by elite sellers. As the tech takes on more of the heavy lifting during appointments, more of the reps' dialogue can be pre-determined, making it easier for the broader team to succeed.

To drive the point home: if the Head of Sales initially thought only the top 5% of reps could navigate a particular scenario, they might not focus on creating scripts and training for it. However, if the tech now enables over 50% of the team to handle this scenario, it's their responsibility to provide the necessary scripts and training.

Finally, pay special attention to those agency-maximizing or "design-from-scratch" experiences. These should replace older methods that required configuring details ahead of time and then explaining them during the appointment. We'll dive deeper into this topic later.

Your team should try to anticipate diverse scenarios and questions that may arise during the sales call. While the Happy Path should focus only on the most critical elements, "primary" scripts also need to be prepared for addressing less frequent but significant questions. This approach ensures that sales reps are prepared to deal with objections without overwhelming the customer with unnecessary information.

Ultimately, the journey from conceptualizing the sales process to crafting an effective script is a nuanced and strategic endeavor that requires a lot of work and refinement. Balance information and persuasion with time limits in a way that will guide the customer seamlessly towards a clear and confident decision that they will feel good about.

Now, we've just given you a cursory overview of script creation for a consultative sales process, but we're going to dive deeper into these steps.

STICK WITH THE NARRATIVE

If the goal is to provide a customer with information and help them to make a decision they feel good about, why is it so important to use a narrative? Why do we recommend encasing your sales pitch in an overarching story?

It's simple, really. If someone asked you for the dates of the Hundred Years' War, or some other equally irrelevant-to-you historical fact that you learned in sixth grade, would you remember?

Probably not. Unless you're a history buff.

What if someone asked you to tell them the plot of a great movie that you saw twenty years ago? Could you give it to them?

Probably so. That's the power of story. It sticks. If you're trying to convey something to someone, there's no better way to do it than to find a good story to deliver the information. Be respectful of the customer by figuring out how to tell the story concisely and memorably, then practice delivering it well.

Do great actors sound fake? No. Why not? Because they have a good story to tell, and they've practiced telling it so many times that it no longer sounds scripted; it sounds authentic. To the audience, it feels like the story is occurring right then and there—in the moment. A sales script is no different. And like a good screenplay, it takes time, research, and revision to get to the final draft.

Even when we sat down to write this chapter, we went back and forth trying to figure out a good story to tell to illustrate what a good story is. (It got ugly. Words were exchanged. It didn't come to blows, but Mike still owes Gregg an apology. He knows what he said.) Why? Because it's hard to tell a good story. And it is *particularly* hard when it's a sales pitch because you need to include real raw data. That means gathering information from many sides—product data, sales numbers, customer experience—and assimilating it all into a replicable, interesting narrative, something that can be practiced and repeated without fail.

A real problem with a lot of sales scripts isn't that they sound fake, it's that no one has done the work on the front end to compile the right sales and customer data. Consequently, the script itself isn't written in a way that can support the rep out in the field. Sales reps get nervous talking to customers, especially if they're new or inexperienced, so if the script they're using doesn't feel authentic, compelling, or well-thought-out, they will abandon it at the first sign of trouble. If the customer pushes back in a way they don't expect, if the conversation about price gets prickly, the rep is going to start winging it, skipping steps, blowing past important conversation points, and things will get messy.

Gregg became the top salesperson at his company in Hawaii because he created a great script and stuck to it. He did not deviate. He knew that the script told a good story. It focused on real pain points and their solutions, and it addressed the objections and questions that most customers would have. He delivered it verbatim and brought in huge numbers as a result.

When Mike joined the team, he followed the process, too. He stuck to the script, and his numbers were incredible.

But here's an almost-true story:

At the same time that Gregg was training Mike, he was also training another new salesperson. We'll call him "Scott" (that's also his actual name, but we won't tell if you won't). Gregg was taking them both on ride-alongs and helping them learn the ropes. While Mike stuck to the script and crushed it, Scott did not. Scott was a great guy, but he worried too much about how he was being perceived. He had sales experience, but he'd never used a script before and resisted doing so. He felt like the script gave prospects the wrong impression.

Because Scott didn't believe in the script, he frequently abandoned it or skipped over parts that he hadn't practiced enough to get comfortable with. Unfortunately, customers could feel his discomfort—his presentation seemed jumpy, not smooth—which made it harder for them to reach a decision point. That was the death knell for Scott.

Even experienced salespeople sometimes feel a resistance to scripts. They think they don't need them, or they treat the script as little more than a rough suggestion, not a process in and of itself.

A script tells a story, but it's also a formula. It has steps that create a natural flow leading to a natural outcome. If salespeople skip steps, then they disrupt the natural flow and make it harder to reach the end goal in a way that feels right to the customer.

By the way, things eventually turned around for poor, willful Scott. Through much ribbing and light teasing (along with a small pocket book about sales), Gregg eventually got him performing much better, sticking to the script, and trusting the process. Scott is a great communicator who truly cares about customers, but he had to learn to get over himself. Once he made the choice to follow the process, he began to excel as a salesman, and he eventually performed in the top 5 percent in the company. It just took him a while to get there.

As a salesperson, you can't let your own awkwardness override doing the right thing. The right thing, in this case, is delivering the message (and the story) that has been predetermined to be effective.

GATHERING YOUR RAW MATERIALS

Let's play pretend for a moment. Suppose we, Mike and Gregg, went to a business with zero existing sales content and tried to create a script from scratch. What would we do?

To start, we would ask about the existing sales process:

- What is the order of events from opportunity until someone decides to buy?

- Whether or not that business thinks so, do we think it is possible, in one interaction, to help a customer make a buying decision?

» If we do think it is possible is, can we present enough information so that they can make a decision they'll be happy with?

» If the answer to that is also yes, how much time do we realistically have to deliver information so the customer's eyes don't glaze over? Half an hour? Forty-five minutes?

Let's suppose we determine that a company's sales reps have thirty minutes to deliver information and help the customer make a purchasing decision. Now, we would clarify what they're selling.

- What is the product or service?

- What are the problems that it solves?

  » Does it save people money?

  » Does it make their factory more efficient?

  » Does it streamline their month-end close process?

  » Does it make their hair grow back?

  » Does it make them look twenty-five again?

We always try to identify the customer's biggest questions or concerns about the product, and narrow it down to a few touchstone concerns. For example, with solar, we learned very quickly that the biggest concerns of our customers were:

- Will this really help me? (Or, what is it exactly that you do?) What is the benefit?

- At a high level, how does everything work? (The customer needs to believe in the benefit before they care about anything else)

- Will my roof leak?

- Is the company going to be around to maintain my warranties?

Our whole sales process focused on these touchpoints. We hit them not just once, but several times throughout the consultative sales process.

For solar, we also knew going in that the customer's biggest objection was usually going to be, "It costs too much," so we touched on affordability early. We walked outside with our customers and looked at their electric meter, drilling down on how much they were already spending on electricity so that those numbers, which were often higher than the cost of our product, were already in their heads. In doing so, we were creating empathy. We were trying to help the customer make a decision that was in their best interest.

Next in our script creation process, we would talk to a bunch of sales managers and salespeople at the company.

- How do you sell this product?

    » What's been working?

    » What hasn't?

If customers really love one specific feature of a product, we would take note of that. That's just more raw material for the script. We would also go on ride-alongs and listen to what takes place during sales calls, and we would try to talk to existing customers to discover their biggest pain points.

Once we had all of the relevant information, we would start to piece together a thirty-minute presentation. In almost every instance, the rough framework of a sales script will look like this:

problem, solution, problem, solution, problem, solution

As we began to build the script, we would refine it. We would act it out together, one of us as the salesperson and one of us as the customer, attempting to approximate how a real conversation between a sales rep and customer might go.

Most of the time, nature is going to dictate the order at which you tackle specific customer problems. Often, one aspect of your solution is helpful for solving another problem later on, and keeping that previous solution in mind will help the customer understand the later solution.

For example, in the solar industry, it wouldn't make sense for a salesperson to start talking about how efficient their solar panels are unless they've already talked to the customer about 1) how solar panels can offset their electricity bill and 2) how there's not always enough room on the customer's roof to generate all the electricity they want.

There's a natural flow. First, talk about how solar panels can offset their bill. Then, talk about how they might not have enough room on their roof to put in the number of panels they need to generate all of the electricity they want. Finally, talk about how efficient your panels are, reducing the number of panels they need to install.

In other words, one "problem > solution" should naturally lead to the next "problem > solution," so you're building a case that will naturally flow into the customer's decision at the end.

Remember, we're not just creating an information dump. We're trying to craft a story, and the value proposition has to be the main character.

Before we move on, a word of caution. We've seen situations where a sales manager developed a sales process that seemed to work well but their sales team struggled to connect with it because the process was written around the manager's personality. To avoid this (or any other framework problems), we recommend sticking with the "problem, solution, problem, solution" formula because even your least gifted sales rep can understand and implement it (even if they lack a charismatic personality).

Ultimately, creating a sales script is no different than writing a book. It's shorter, and you get to say it out loud, but the goal is the same: tell a good story and convey an idea so it's easy to absorb.

Let's take an insider's view into a compelling story-driven sales process, so you can go out and replicate it for your own product and team.

CRAFTING YOUR SCRIPT

BUILD RAPPORT

Before your sales reps jump into talking about your product (which is a mistake they often make), you have to start by building rapport. This shouldn't be done off the cuff. It should be part of your sales script. In solar, we usually conducted sales calls in people's homes, so we always started with a walk-around during which we complimented things about the home that we noticed and liked.

As the sales rep is walking around a customer's house or office during this early part of the process, observe what's around. Are they really into cars? Do they surf? Are there pictures of interesting trips they've taken all over the walls? Pay attention. Ask questions. If you're not interested in what they're interested in, at least be open and curious enough to want to find out more.

We let the homeowners know if we thought their home was a good candidate for solar, and we asked them if there was a part of their roof they thought might work for solar panels. Right away, it was a conversation. They were involved and engaged, and we were building familiarity.

Then we walked over to their electric meter. We explained how it worked, talking about usage and customization, and we explained things like kilowatt hours. We explained how they get charged, and we told them that when we put solar panels on the roof, they were going to make the meter, in essence, spin backwards.

Depending on the market, we might say something like, "For every kilowatt hour we spin that meter backwards, you'll get a credit. At night, when the sun goes down, you'll use that power, but you'll use it for free. Does that make sense?"

It was a genuinely exciting idea for most people. This was still part of our script, but it felt like we were just talking. We were building rapport, but already we were starting to address some of the major touchpoints. Remember, this was all part of our sales script. Sales reps weren't winging it or "just chatting."

Part of the reason we took customers to the meter was because understanding energy output and cost savings was one of the more complicated aspects of our product. If we spent some time looking at the meter and talking about how it all worked, then when we got to those details in the presentation, customers would already have a bit of familiarity.

Look for similar patterns when building your script, concepts or details that should be brought up several times so customers understand them when you return to those topics later on in the script.

When you're creating your script, home in on the elements of your product or industry that are complicated and think about ways you can casually build understanding very early on. Even if the customer tells the sales rep they already understand these elements, the rep needs to do a good job of explaining them anyway. Maybe the customer spoke to another sales rep previously who has already explained these things. Assume the previous sales rep didn't do a thorough job, or left out some key information, and explain it better.

You want to ensure that the customer truly understands what the rep is talking about because later parts of the script may depend on the nuance of what they're conveying earlier. In fact, they might need to hit on those topics quite a few times in order to create enough familiarity that, when it's time to make a decision, the customer can do it in an informed way.

For example, we talked a lot about financing when it came to solar installation, and for some people this information was just not digestible. If we started throwing out APR and rate terms too quickly, their eyes would glaze over—so we didn't talk about things like that all at once. Instead, we talked about what they were already paying, and then we showed them another way to pay for it, and slowly brought in more and more details about financing until the customers could make solid decisions they would be happy with.

We identified the problem: They were going to wind up paying $125,000 (or whatever it may be) for electricity over the next twenty years.

Then we offered a solution: When we came out and put solar panels on the roof, it was going to conceptually spin the meter backwards and may save them X amount of money.

That's a story they can understand, with no gobbledygook.

The sales rep can use a bit of Socratic dialogue, where they ask the customer a series of questions that prompt the customer to clarify their problems and identify their solution for themselves. This is not the same as leading questions, because you're not forcing the customer to give you a specific answer in order to avoid looking foolish. Rather, the Socratic approach assumes the customer already has the truth within them (about the right solution), and you're simply prompting them to draw it out and see if it aligns with *your* solution.

Socratic questions flow logically from the information that has already been given, and if done well, build trust and rapport. So, for example, the sales rep could start with something like, "So, you told me on the phone when we scheduled this meeting that your energy bills are super high these days. Why do you think they've gotten so high?" The customer is being prompted to clarify their own problem, which the rep can then build on with a series of questions that lead them to reveal the solution themselves.

That said, a good script will guide a sales rep through much of this work. If the sales process is solid, it will build rapport all on its own. Once the rep understands the process, they don't have to spend a lot of time looking for ways to connect. They just have to go through the process and be polite, respectful, and engaging, pay attention to the customer, and listen carefully.

No matter what, the sales rep's job is to approach this early conversation with respect and humility. That's the number one way to build rapport. Their thought process should be, "I believe so much in my product and my company that I'm surprised when people say no—but I'm not hurt by it. Our value proposition is excellent, so if I do a good job delivering the script and answering the questions that arise, I'm going to assume we'll proceed— not because I must have a sale at all costs, but because I haven't yet learned any reason why this won't be a good solution to the customer's problem." That's a respectful yet confident position. That's a person customers can trust.

SEEK MUTUAL UNDERSTANDING

Once the sales rep has built rapport, it's time for them and the customer to seek mutual understanding.

Let's be crystal clear about this. The sales rep should not try to force agreement. Ever. They're not trying to back the customer into a corner using leading questions. If they're early in the sales process and a customer is freaked out by the cost, that's perfectly fine. All it means is that the rep has discovered something about the customer's scenario that makes what they have to offer not a good fit. The customer doesn't value the solution enough, or they don't have the typical pain points of other customers. Whatever it is, the rep and customer have figured it out together and come to a mutual understanding—and that's always a good thing.

Consultative sales is by definition a complicated process, and you want the customer not to get confused as the sales appointment unfolds. At every step, the sales rep should seek understanding. Things need to make sense to the customer now so the rep can help them make a decision later.

Throughout the sales process, this is going to be the approach:

1. Give an explanation,

2. Ask if it makes sense,

3. Don't move on until there's mutual understanding.

One of the great things about a script-based consultative sales process is that the sales rep isn't forced to think on their feet all the time. They can deliver a message they know is useful, but they don't have to think too hard to deliver it because they've practiced. They know it by heart. This frees them up to pay attention to the most important thing in any sales process: the other person.

Sales reps should practice **active listening** by not merely hearing the customer's words but observing their facial expressions and underlying emotions. Sometimes, these nonverbal forms of communication are the only way a customer will reveal that they didn't understand something or are having some concern.

"Buyers are liars" is a saying that refers to the supposed fact that customers often say they want one thing but end up buying something else. In practice, the saying is used to justify pushing products onto customers with no regard for what they actually need. Ironically, it then becomes a self-fulfilling prophecy. Customers who have been subjected to this kind of approach tend to keep their cards close to the vest because they don't want to be abused again. They no longer trust sales, so they may indeed lie to the sales rep.

It's a crappy approach to sales. A good sales process shows a customer that the rep actually cares about their input and represents their wishes. It builds trust, which leads to a dramatic growth in referral sales. It's just better all around.

Again, it's important to pay attention to those nonverbal cues. Humans are incredibly adept at determining when someone they're talking to is confused or not on the same page; take advantage of that fact and create situations where reps can allow that human tendency to shine. Set yourself up for success by having a process that allows your sales team to simply deliver the script so they can focus on active listening. Then they'll know for sure when it's landing, and when it's not. And when it's not, they can adjust, not by going rogue but by drilling down into the script that already exists.

Sales reps should explain the product exactly as scripted (and practiced), but when they see that the understanding isn't there, they can try to explain the same point in a slightly different way, and keep coming back to that need for mutual understanding by telling the customer, "I'm sorry, I don't think I did a good job explaining that; let me try another way." Remember, the information they're conveying to the customer early on is going to be instrumental in the customer making a decision they can be happy with later.

Make things easy and straightforward. The customer has a problem, and the sales rep is there to provide a solution. The customer won't hear that solution if the rep has over-complicated things right out of the gate. This starts with the simplest, smallest details.

Many sales reps feel they have to overcompensate in order to be perceived as experts, so they use a lot of esoteric language and technical terms designed to make them sound super smart. This is ego-driven sales, and it doesn't help them build trust with customers. If a sales rep follows a well-scripted process, simply and clearly communicating a value proposition that meets the customer's needs, then both parties win. Yes, they definitely need to know the product well enough to communicate why it's better than competitors, but they should do it in a clear, concise manner that customers understand. For example, at Sunpro, we used to say "sun power" and "home power" instead of DC and AC electricity because it required less explanation and instantly clicked for the customer.

Gregg once had a sales meeting with an MIT professor working on next-gen solar cells to improve panel efficiency. Imagine if Gregg had tried to act like a solar panel expert in that meeting—it probably wouldn't have gone well. Instead, he stuck to the script and provided a product spec sheet. Afterward, the MIT professor complimented him on how simply he had communicated the product's value, and he wound up purchasing from the company, even though the product was priced higher than the competition by a significant margin.

Of course, a sales rep can only rely on the script to provide the expertise if the script has all of the right relevant information. On another occasion, Gregg had a sales meeting with a man named Mr. Nakagami. As he made his sales presentation, Mr. Nakagami listened with his arms crossed, leaning back in his chair. He nodded at everything Gregg said. Things seemed to be going well, so when Gregg got to the end of his presentation, he asked Mr. Nakagami, "Does an installation date of June 15th or August 12th work best for you?"

And Mr. Nakagami leaned forward in his chair and said, "I'm not buying from you today. I'm not buying from you ever."

Gregg was shocked. "Why?"

"Because," said Mr. Nakagami, "you disrespected me."

More shock. "How?" Gregg asked. "How did I do that?"

Mr. Nakagami pointed at Gregg's presentation documents. "You got my name wrong on your document there. It's not Nakagami. It's Nakayoshi."

Gregg knew there was nothing he could do to save that sale. He left with his stomach full of humble pie. That mistake made him realize how important it is to have the right information, so the next time he started a sales process with a customer, he added a step:

"Before we get started," he asked, "do I have everything spelled correctly here?"

This became page one of the Sunpro sales process. We started getting agreement on names and correct spelling before we did anything else. Not only did this prevent an unintentional insult, but it also sped up the process down the road. If their name is spelled wrong, financing won't go through. When a sales rep is working in a market with a lot of red tape, or where customer service is notoriously difficult, they can let the customer know, "We do these double-checks so that when we submit permits and financing documents, everything will move exponentially faster."

All of a sudden, they've established themselves as someone who cares. They're paying attention. They want to get things right and create understanding right out of the gate. A customer is going to see that, and it's going to mean something to them.

This is especially true when the sales rep and the customer are looking at a presentation on paper (or on a screen) together. What they see should be as easy to understand as what they hear. Their name needs to be correct, their numbers need to be correct, so double-check all of your information when preparing for the sales call.

Additionally, the rep should not overwhelm them with information. When you're trained in giving technical presentations, one of the first things you're taught is to avoid putting a bunch of text on a slide because people are going to start reading and they'll stop listening to you. It's the same when you have visual sales tools, whether that's an old fashioned pitch book or an application that stands in as a virtual pitch book. Make sure whatever is visible in the application is pared down so that ideally only information relevant to the current topic is visible—nothing else to distract.

PROBLEM, SOLUTION, PROBLEM, SOLUTION

By now, you've established rapport, you've built some trust and understanding, now it's time to focus on the customer's pain points.

Using our solar scenario, remember that we've already identified a few major pain points for our target customers, including:

- How much does it cost?

- Will my roof leak?

- Is the company going to be around to maintain my warranties?

During our walk-around, we already discussed the fact that the customer is going to be paying $125,000 in utility bills over the next twenty years. We said something like, "Wow, that's a lot, isn't it?" to get the customer to acknowledge that this is a lot of money. Then we told the customer that solar is often significantly less than that. We were careful to make sure that this claim was extremely accurate and added some caveats so we were never overpromising.

Notice, we were focusing on the pain point, which was the huge amount of money they were going to be shelling out. Salespeople usually want to focus on solutions right away. They want to talk about their product's features and benefits, but none of that is going to land with a customer if you don't first strongly underline the pain points.

Problem first, then solution. Next problem, next solution. And so on.

If the sale involves an ROI element that the customer might not understand without covering some basics first, the rep should always start with those fundamentals. Great sales leaders crafting effective scripts anticipate topics that could lead to pushback and find ways to prepare the customer during the call, so they're ready to face the realities of their decision. In solar sales, for example, if the customer is buying with a loan, the script should mention the "cost of doing nothing" multiple times, comparing it to the loan amount. This helps the customer make a more rational decision.

The sales rep should stay focused on the value proposition of the product (which is really just another way of thinking about "problem, solution"). When they do that, they can walk away from the sales meeting clean, no matter what the customer decides. Their job is simply to present the information and help the customer make a decision that is in their own best interest.

If the customer's circumstances are such that they're not going to see the savings or experience the benefits of the product, then the sales rep doesn't need to try to jam a square peg into a round hole. They should simply thank the customer for their time, ask for a referral, and be on their way. Asking for a referral should go something like this: "Is there anyone else you know that would benefit from this solution?" Put this in the script! It is not an off-the-cuff request but part of your consultative sales process. In fact, a referral program should be mentioned upfront so that the customer understands the benefits of the program before the rep even asks.

Generally, after talking about how solar panels would offset the customer's electricity bill, customers wanted to know about their roof. "How many panels will have to go up there? Will the roof leak?" This was a natural concern because we were about to bore holes in probably their biggest investment (their home).

At this point, we would often show some pictures contrasting the difference between the way our company installed panels with some examples of poorly-installed panels. We didn't call out the other companies by name, just highlighted the differences. This was always a highly effective technique because it addressed this major pain point with customers in a dramatic and visual way.

Prevent objections by making sure the customer truly understands key points. If your offering is more expensive than the competition, find a way for the sales rep to highlight the value your product delivers. Some customers might not mind a lower-quality option, but others will. Only by the sales rep making this clear can the customer make an informed decision.

Often, he would hand them one of the metal flashings used for installation and show them how impossible it would be for water to move up the side of the flashing and get in their roof.

The end of this part of the script might go something like, "Now that you understand how we install, another common question is, 'Will this impact my roof warranty?'" The sales rep should be equipped with scripts, processes, and software to clearly explain their solution to this problem.

Thus far, every "problem > solution" has flowed naturally out of the one before. From there, the customer might have additional questions. They might want to know more about the specifics of the installation, the "before and after." This is why the sales rep needs to have as much information as possible available right at their fingertips in those "primary objection" scripts. They have to be ready to discuss the details if the customer asks for more information.

As you're building your script, always stay in the cadence of *problem, solution, problem, solution,* with each problem/solution leading naturally into the next problem/solution. The sales rep's goal is to stick to the Happy Path as much as possible but be ready to answer those primary questions if the customer brings them up.

In solar, no customer cared if our Standard Test Conditions ratings were high. They cared about how the solar panels were going to save them money and justify their investment. They cared about the condition of their roof, and they cared about why our product was better than a competitor down the street.

When it comes to your own product, what do your customers actually care about? What truly matters to them?

Make sure you understand the competitive landscape. What are the pros and cons of your competitors, and how can you position yourself against them?

TO RECAP

A good sales script tells a good story, and it supports salespeople out in the field. It takes considerable prep work before that story can be told well, but it's so worth it. The script becomes the backbone of the entire sales process, so take the time and the effort to make it high-quality and empathetic, and make the team rehearse it until it's part of their DNA. Everyone involved in sales, from the reps to whoever is at the very top of sales leadership ladder in your company, should know the sales script by heart and be able to recite it from memory.

Even if the sales rep does all of this well, the customer may still have some objections. They may have some variation of, "This sounds like a good product/service, but..." Your sales reps need to be ready to address these objections before they can close a deal.

A good sales script:

- Builds rapport with the customer

- Proactively addresses the most common questions and pain points that your product solves using a natural flow of "problem, solution, problem, solution"

- Presents enough information that the customer can make a decision to purchase or not to purchase and be happy with the results

- Gives the salesperson the tools to address questions and alleviate customer objections

That final bullet point is incredibly important. Remember, the Happy Path script is going to preemptively address the most common objections customers might raise, but sales reps also need scripts to deal with those less common "primary" objections. In fact, handling objections can be a tricky process, so let's look at it in more detail.

CHAPTER THREE

HANDLING OBJECTIONS

The best way to deal with an objection is to prevent it from happening in the first place.

One of the benefits of having a good script is that it means you've thought a lot about all of the common questions that customers are going to ask, and you've addressed them in your Happy Path (or default) script. This ensures along the way that the customer understands each point the sales rep makes. So, for example, the rep makes their first point, and then they ask, "Did I explain that clearly?" If the customer answers in the affirmative, the rep can move on to Point B, and then ask again, "Did I explain that clearly enough?" They keep doing that as they move through the "problem, solution" cadence.

But maybe the customer asks the rep a question in the middle of Point B that the rep knows they're going to address later on in the Happy Path script. Instead of deviating or letting their presentation get derailed, the rep can simply say, "That's a great question. I'm going to get to that a little bit later. I need to provide you with some other information first to really help make sure I do a good job of explaining how all this works. Is it okay if I answer a bit later?" The rep should aim to make the customer feel good about asking a question—because then the customer will be encouraged to ask more throughout the sales call—then promise to get to it later and return to the script.

We've never heard a customer say no to that question, but if they do, the rep can quickly deviate, answer their question, then jump right back into Point B.

A good script spares the rep from having to address every objection on the fly and preserves the logical flow of "problem, solution, problem, solution." That's why you need to make sure your script does a good job of keeping them on the Happy Path, proactively dealing with the most common questions you know customers will have while also providing effective responses for less common objections.

You don't want to create a situation where you never allow customers to make any real objections, where the rep just keeps barreling forward on their predetermined path no matter what. Yes, there are some high-energy salespeople who operate this way. Somehow, they seem to close deals left and right with a take-no-prisoners approach. But high pressure tactics harm the relationship between sales rep and customer, and the customer's ongoing relationship with the company suffers. The sales rep might make themselves look great, but the operational team is often left holding the bag of promises the rep made to get the sale.

Just because a customer wasn't allowed to voice real objections doesn't mean there weren't any, and those objections are going to come out eventually. When they do, that cancel lever is going to get pulled. The customer may not bother to say no during the sales call because they want the sales rep and his or her insane energy out of their house, but they may say no later.

Selling in Hawaii was a great training ground for developing a better and more respectful approach, because high-energy sales are not welcome in Hawaii. There, the "power of the pause" is key. In other words, we learned to trust the process, which means we had to learn how to hold, wait, and pause so our customers could be seen, heard, and understood.

This isn't exclusive to Hawaii. Customers everywhere want to feel seen, heard, and understood. If sales reps are just there to blow past their concerns, get in and get out, they're not going to accomplish anything long term. So the first thing we would say about dealing with objections is this:

The sales rep's posture should be one of listening, understanding, and empathizing.

THEIR CONCERN IS YOUR CONCERN

As a consumer, have you ever felt like a price point was too high? Or that you needed more information about the competition before you purchased a product? We all have. And how does it make you feel when a sales rep blows by your concern? It's irritating, isn't it?

When customers feel disrespected by a sales rep, when they feel like their concerns are being sidestepped, they may start lying to the sales reps just to get them to shut up, so they can leave and go buy from a cheaper competitor. When a customer is determined to get a sales rep out of their sight, they will say whatever they can to get away from them.

Clearly, that's not what you want. When a customer brings up their concerns, they should feel like the rep gets it; that they appreciate where the customer is coming from. Sales reps must learn how to tap into a customer's emotions, to empathize with them and not just sympathize.

If a customer expresses a concern that the price is too high, the sales rep should try to understand how they feel. Maybe the rep has been in a similar situation themselves. Maybe they can remember a time when they felt a price was too high. How did they feel, and how did they want the sales rep to respond?

Sales reps need to learn how to get themselves on the customer's side of the negotiation table. See things from their perspective. Once you do that, the customer will usually let their guard down, and that's when the real conversation begins.

When the rep approaches customers from a place of empathy, they intuitively feel that the rep is on their side. And when the rep is willing to admit that other customers have had similar concerns, the customer is going to feel understood and validated.

It only takes seconds to make a customer feel listened to, and just a few more seconds to make sure you've come to a mutual understanding before moving on.

Many salespeople are so worried about letting a sale slip away that they "white knuckle" it, but selling demands patience. They should fight the urge to jump ahead in order to overcome the objection, and instead, ask clarifying questions like, "When you say the price is too high, what do you mean by that?"

The sales rep has to be willing to lose the sale. They should use an open hand, not a closed fist, and trust the process so much that they're okay if they and the customer realize together that it's not a good fit. If they try to force a sale by rushing through the customer's concerns, they're going to blow the whole thing. The sales rep needs to let the customer hang out in that space for a bit instead of trying to pummel them with objections to their objections just so the rep can hurry up and get back to their presentation. Encourage your reps to pause, take a deep breath, and trust the process. And if it's not a good fit, learn from the experience. Maybe they'll find there's a better way to address that objection in the future.

Let's suppose the customer says the price is too high. How should the rep respond? Some salespeople might respond aggressively in order to get back on track as soon as possible:

"Too high?! We're the number one solar company in the business, and we sell a top tier product! Of course we cost more than the competition."

At this point, many sales reps would attempt to speak negatively about the competition, but the customer will not care about anything the rep has to say until they acknowledge the customer's concern. The sales rep should first try to understand what they mean by "the price is too high."

They can say something like, "By 'too expensive,' what do you mean?'"

The rep will learn something over the course of the conversation if they simply let the customer hang out there for a moment. Chances are that they need to do a better job of communicating the real value of the product—an insight that allows you to refine your consultative sales process moving forward.

In any sales presentation there are going to be hills and valleys. That's life. So the rep should allow the customer to explore the valleys. If they don't, even if they manage to force one sale, the company's customer satisfaction will plummet.

When sales reps gloss over problems, they invalidate the customer's feelings. Sales reps should give the customer space and let them tell the rep more about their concerns. What they share with the rep might be absolute gold that they can use to become more effective.

Let's take a closer look at how sales reps should handle customer objections.

1. CLARIFY THE CONCERN

Once the customer has expressed a concern, the rep's first step is to clarify what they mean. First, they should shift their language from "objection" to "concern." An objection is adversarial, something to be tackled head-on and defeated. When the rep sees it as an objection, their natural tendency is to adopt a fighting stance. But they're not trying to ju-jitsu their way past them; they're trying to help and serve them.

A *concern* allows the rep to empathize and listen, which is something most sales reps don't do well. Yes, they may have heard the same objection a hundred times before, but they shouldn't just rush to their preplanned answer so they can hurry past it. Encourage them to take a breath, then respond with empathy. How the rep responds to a concern could make all the difference in getting the customer to a decision they feel good about.

When a customer brings up a concern, the rep should first ask for clarification.

"The price seems too high."

"By 'price too high,' what do you mean?"

Asking this question with an open and curious mind builds connection. Make sure the rep doesn't assume they already know the answer, even if they've heard it many times before from other customers. And don't try to overcome the objection yet. Trust the process!

2. AGREE, AGREE, AGREE

Once the customer has expressed their concern and clarified what they mean, the rep needs to agree with the *reason* for their concern. The rep doesn't have to agree that the price is too high, but they should agree that the customer's concern is legitimate—it's real to them.

If the customer points out that your product costs more than the competition, the rep can say something like, "That *is* a significant difference, isn't it?"

Empathy must come before the solution! The rep should let the customer know that they understand why the customer is asking the question, and should celebrate their smart thinking. They should also fight the temptation to rush ahead—not to be afraid to walk through the valley of the shadow of sales death with the customer, as long as they're leading the customer to a decision that will feel *right*.

The rep should allow the uncomfortable feeling to linger. Yes, they might be able to crush the customer's objection ruthlessly, but they need to remember that they're in the learning stage, and they're also preserving the customer's sense of autonomy. Clearly, something didn't click.

Now, the truth is, many of the customer's objections should be handled proactively during the rep's presentation. If they get all the way to the discussion on financing and a customer says, "I'm not sure how I'm going to come up with the money for this," then the rep has done something wrong in creating their default script. They should have already covered cost savings and financing options in the Happy Path script.

If an objection is likely to come up 5-50% of the time, you should have scripts ready for your reps. However, you'll need to decide if this should replace something else, as there's only so much time in a sales call. For objections expected less than 5% of the time, it's up to you to decide if creating scripts, training, and collateral is worth the effort.

This step in the sales process—agreeing with the customer's concern—is what separates the good reps from the great! Above all, the goal at this point is to show the customer that the rep cares rather than just trying to rush them over the finish line. If they don't explore the discomfort, concern, and perhaps misunderstanding, and work through it, it reduces customer engagement and lowers their perception of the seller, the company, or both. This can lead to higher customer service costs if the customer does buy, and lower conversion rates if they don't.

Encourage reps to walk through the valley with the customer! Allow them to express concerns, while the rep listens carefully and then shows them why your product is worth the higher price. And if it's a misunderstanding, they can help clarify that misunderstanding.

3. ADDRESS THE CONCERN

At this point, the rep has sat with your customer in the "valley of death," they've allowed the customer to express their concerns, and they've done their best to make them feel heard and understood. Finally, it is time to move to the appropriate "primary objection" script that they've been trained on in order to address and overcome that specific objection. They need to respond to the objection effectively and powerfully so the customer will either come out of the valley thinking differently or at least have crystal clarity.

To use our previous example, let's suppose the customer has told the rep that the price is too high. The rep responded by asking what they mean, and they've replied, "There's a huge difference between your price quote and a competitor's price quote."

The rep now needs to learn what the competitor is offering that makes the price seem too high. Often, a customer may *think* both products are the same, but there could be significant differences that account for the higher price. One way the rep could address this would be to approach it with genuine curiosity: "We're both reputable solar companies. We get good reviews, and we have high customer satisfaction, so there must be a reasonable explanation for the price difference. Let's see if we can figure out why."

They can pause a moment to let their initial response sink in.

Then they can ask some specific questions about the competitor's proposal to try to discover the difference. The customer may even go and get the proposal and bring it to the rep, so they can look at it together.

In this, the rep has created a compelling response using two key pieces of information:

1. Your product is well worth the higher price, and

2. There must be some real difference between what you offer and what your competitor offers that explains (and justifies) the price difference.

Now, instead of the customer thinking the price is too high, they're wondering, "Why are these two offerings at such a different price?" instead of simply thinking, "The price is too high." By the way, the rep should word this such that everybody is given the benefit of the doubt. It may be true that something is genuinely wrong with the competition, but chances are the customer thinks both products are offering the same thing when, in fact, the products are different.

If the customer goes and gets the other proposal, they and the rep can look it over together to find and explain the differences, and ultimately verify that the more expensive product is actually more valuable in a way that is worthwhile to the customer.

This changes the sales rep's position from defending their price to demonstrating excellence in the price difference. The subtext being communicated is, "There is no way we would be able to perform the same amazing service for a lower price. We use high quality products, and we honor our warranties."

This approach is applicable for any good company. You don't actually have to be the best company in your industry to justify your higher price point. There may be other reasons. The sales rep should explore them with the customer, and encourage the customer to Google some reviews and look at what people are saying about your competitor.

Maybe the reason for the difference is that you're a decent company that charges enough money to stay in business, pay your people a fair wage, and serve your clients when things go wrong. If someone else is offering a similar product for significantly less, it's likely that they're either cutting corners, or not doing business in a way that will keep them financially viable.

The rep's goal is to show the customer what the differences are and attach a dollar value to each difference. At this point the price difference should be clearly seen and stated. (As you'll see in the coming chapters, this is where great tech can really make a difference.)

Whatever the rep does, their response to the customer's objection needs to be *memorable* and *authentic*. They need to change the customer's thinking with it.

And, by the way, if reps keep running into the same objection with customer after customer, then maybe there's something wrong with your company that you need to fix. Maybe your prices really are too high! There may be a real, legitimate problem that needs to be confronted in-house.

If you control your own sales enablement application, you can create highly optimized user experiences to address objections. At Sunpro, our sales call plan led with the most efficient panels, which often meant our sales reps encountered customers with competing proposals offering similar panel counts but at a lower total price. To handle this, we designed user experiences within our enablement app that made it easy for even new reps to explain the differences. They could show that, although panel counts were similar, the total energy produced by less efficient systems was lower (like comparing quotes for ten 100W bulbs vs. ten 60W bulbs—the same quantity but different outputs).

Our sales reps could simply tap a few buttons to make all the differences visible, allowing customers to decide whether they preferred the higher-efficiency panels or a different option. Gregg and Mike, along with their teams, continually collaborated on field objections and learned how top-performing reps with satisfied customers handled these situations. They translated this knowledge into user experiences within the app so new reps could replicate those approaches. With control over your own sales enablement solution, your process becomes: gather insights from an elite seller today, and make that the standard plan for all reps by tomorrow!

4. RETURN TO UNDERSTANDING

Once the rep has addressed the objection, they need to confirm that the customer understands so they can move from the objection script back to the Happy Path. In our example, this is as easy as very carefully stating something like, "Oh, I see why their pricing is less. Look here. We use high efficiency products, while they have standard efficiency products." Or, "They are not offering a service warranty, but we are. Would you like me to remove it or keep it as it is?" Or, "We pay our installation crew very well. This is why we have such high customer satisfaction." Or whatever the case may be.

And then finish by saying, "Does that make sense?"

This question drives the customer to either agree or disagree with you. It's very powerful if they agree, in which case, you can move on. If not, then you must dig back into the point of confusion, clarify it, and ask again.

You have to wait for this confirmation. Again, there is power in the pause. If you ask a question and don't wait for the answer, then the customer is going to think you don't value what they have to say. Resist the urge to keep talking. People who ramble on do not walk with influence or purpose. Don't be that person! Every word out of place devalues your message and devalues the person saying it. So don't budge until you get your answer.

Wait!

If the customer won't answer then everything you did before was a waste of time. They may have more objections, especially if it's a complex issue. If that's the case, keep repeating the steps above until you're able to get to understanding.

Or you might find that the customer just doesn't care about the specifics. They don't care if your competitor is shoddily run or about to go out of business. Their product is cheaper, and that's all that matters to them. If that's the case, don't be upset, and don't be a smart ass about it. Wish the customer well and let them know you get it. They are simply not your customer, and that's okay.

Some customers only care about the lowest pricing, and highly trained installers or a higher quality product are not important to them. Remember, there are people who bought Yugo cars in the mid-80s and thought it was a sound purchase. Pack up and go on your merry way. The customer made a decision they feel good about, with a sense of autonomy, and that's what you're after.

Never forget: A salesperson is in the decision-making business. The only acceptable outcomes are "yes," "no," or an *exact* time and date to meet again (e.g., This Friday at 2pm). If the customer says, "I'll talk to you later, after I think about it," with no commitment to a specific time or date to meet again, then the sales rep did not do their duty. They should dig in to find out why.

Or if the customer refuses to answer, we recommend asking, "If you had to make a decision between our company and the competitor's company, which would be the best fit?" This will almost always bring the client to the real reason they can't decide.

And if the customer has more questions or concerns before they can get to that decision, that's good, too. The more the rep can make them feel seen, heard, and understood, the better. How does the rep know if they've done that well? Because the customer has said yes or no—or they've agreed on a specific time and date to meet again.

5. MOVE ON

There is power in moving on. Once the customer has acknowledged that the sales rep has overcome their objection, the rep should avoid going back, asking more questions, or continuing to explain why the company is great. Move on. The customer is done with it, and so should the rep be. The rep is out of the valley and should proceed to the next part of the process.

Too many salespeople feel the need to revisit the objection just to make sure, but this only makes the customer feel like the rep didn't truly listen. The rep asked if the customer understood the response, and the customer said yes. So why go back and try to overcome the objection again? When the customer says they're good, the rep should believe them.

To summarize, when dealing with an objection, the rep should:

1. Clarify the concern,

2. Agree with the customer's feelings,

3. Address the concern,

4. Return to understanding,

5. Then move on!

The rep's goal is *always* to help the customer make a good decision. In the end, that's the only approach worth taking.

PART TWO

TWO

THE TECH

CHAPTER FOUR

WHY YOU NEED
A CUSTOMIZED SALES TOOL

There are plenty of off-the-shelf sales tools on the market, and many of them are great for solving certain problems.

However, if you can make the investment, nothing is going to make a greater impact on your sales performance than a customized sales enablement tool. Nothing. At Sunpro, the internally developed sales enablement application began as a strategic initiative and evolved into a mission-critical tool, becoming a powerful asset in competitive markets nationwide. Four years after its launch, Sunpro reached $1 billion in annualized book sales, with $83.3 million booked in a single month, after doubling in size four years in a row. The CEO believes that without this application, Sunpro would not have achieved this growth.

So what exactly can custom sales tech do for you that off-the-shelf software can't do? How does it improve the sales process? It's a big investment, so it needs to have a big payoff, right? Of course. Let's clarify the value it can deliver.

Generally, the more complex a sale is, the longer the sales cycle tends to be. This is primarily due to the increased number of variables that need to be addressed or optimized by the sales rep in order to not need to use pushy close tactics to get a decision from the customer.

To illustrate this, consider the example of buying bubblegum from a store. The only variable in this scenario is whether the store has the bubblegum or not. Once this is confirmed, the decision to purchase is made. This is a simple sale with a short sales cycle.

On the other end of the spectrum, consider the example of an airline needing to overhaul its fleet and order twelve new jumbo airliners. This decision involves hundreds of thousands of variables such as the routes, the cost of parts, hundreds of stakeholders, dozens of decision makers, the color of the planes, and so on. This is a complex sale with a long sales cycle.

The relationship between the number of variables optimized and the value delivered when someone makes a purchasing decision is critical. If a decision is made too quickly without considering enough variables, the buyer may not be satisfied with their decision. They might realize after the fact that they missed out on options they would have preferred. If pushy tactics were used to make the sale, they may feel negatively towards the company after they become a customer.

Sales reps are generally incentivized to address *just enough variables* to get someone to make a purchasing decision. However, the more variables that can be optimized by the time a customer makes a decision, the more value ultimately ends up being delivered to the customer. This is because, *after* making a decision, customers often continue to learn more and realize additional needs or preferences they may have. Also, to get a customer to make a decision despite an unaddressed variable, a sales rep may use a pushy tactic (a hard close). In such cases, the buyer often retains hard feelings toward the rep, the organization, or both after the purchase.

This learning process can lead to increased costs for the seller due to increased customer support costs, a higher likelihood of cancellation, and decreased value over time as the customer refers less business and becomes more expensive to manage.

Customized sales tech can help in this scenario by allowing a sales rep to optimize more variables in the same amount of time. This means that when a customer makes a decision, they are further along the value delivery curve. The technology helps push them up and to the right on the chart of variables optimized versus value delivered, addressing more variables during the time spent with the customer.

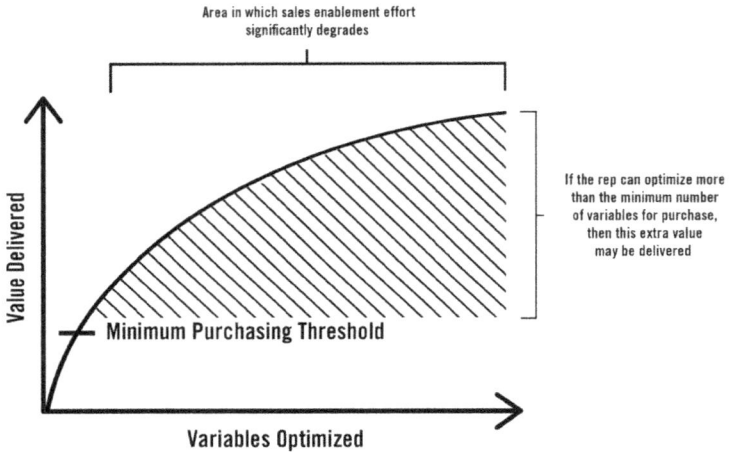

If more variables for a customer's solution are addressed in a manner where the customer has more agency, they will receive more value. As we've discussed, humans inherently resist making a purchase if they feel like their sense of agency is compromised. As they gain more agency, they become more receptive to the value of what is being sold.

If sales technology is applied correctly, it can optimize for both customer agency and value delivery. This dual optimization is not an obvious outcome, but when achieved, it results in a dramatically better-performing middle class of sales reps.

So let's summarize. How does customized sales tech make a difference?

- **First,** by enabling reps to address more variables in a sales meeting, which moves customers further up the value delivery curve when they make their decision.

- And **second,** by creating situations where there's increased customer agency, which in turn lowers their resistance to receiving value.

If you're having a hard time wrapping your head around these advantages of using customized sales enablement software, here's an example from our own solar sales experience.

To create the Sales Call (the topics and scripts to be used), we start with the essential topics that need to be covered. Then we consider the characteristics of each topic, such as:

- Is it likely to trigger customer reluctance (e.g., "We'll need to check your credit now," or "Let's fill out the paperwork now")?

- Is it prone to causing discord for the rep (e.g., a rep selling a leased system when they would never lease a car themselves)?

- Is it difficult to comprehend?

- Does it require a decision from the customer?

- Does it involve explaining a decision we made before the Sales Call (e.g., a configuration based on assumptions explained during the call)?

We then focus on how to improve the overall Sales Call experience.

If a topic is likely to cause customer reluctance, we may introduce it several times to prepare the customer for addressing it fully later in the call. If a topic is prone to discord for the rep, we might add a feature that slows down the process, presenting the value proposition in an explicit, step-by-step manner through multiple screens or interactions that the rep and customer navigate together.

If the topic is hard to understand, we might use a mix of approaches from the previous examples but with a focus on clarity. For topics requiring a decision, we might create features that help the customer make a choice that aligns with their best interest, perhaps by making the decision's implications extra clear.

For topics involving a decision we made before the Sales Call, we might add features that create a "design-from-scratch" experience with the customer. This approach allows the customer to reach the same configuration or design through their own choices during the call, even if we based it on our initial assumptions as sellers.

For example, during a sales conversation, our rep would bring up a visual of a solar power system designed to meet the customer's needs. This image was interactive, allowing adjustments on the fly based on the customer's input.

The rep might ask, "Do you have a preference for where the panels should go?"

The customer might respond, "I want them here, where I won't see them when I drive up to my home," and point to a part of the roof on the screen. The rep would then press a button, and the panels would appear on the image exactly where the customer indicated.

"Great! This part of your home doesn't get as much sunshine as other areas, so we'd need to add more panels to offset your utility bill. This will make the system more expensive, but I can show you the exact price difference when we get to that part. Sound good?"

"Well, in that case," the customer might say, "let's use the sunnier parts of my home. I think I could get used to seeing the panels when I drive up."

With a simple user experience, the solar panels would then move to the sunnier parts of the home on the screen.

Or the customer might say, "If it's just a little more expensive, I'd rather not see the panels." The customer may respond in other ways, but the point is that the product manager and sales leader should expect technology to enable these kinds of interactions.

Often, companies don't consider customer preferences in this way because they lack the knowledge or imagination to create such technology. As a result, sales leaders may view these customer questions as "cans of worms" best left unopened. In some cases, companies understand the value of tailoring solutions based on the Sales Call but may only offer "kits" or pre-configured options because they haven't embraced the concepts in this book.

Those mini-interactions might take a mere two minutes out of the total forty-minute sales process. It's fast, easy, and responsive in a way that off-the-shelf software rarely is. More importantly, it gets the customer involved in creating their own solution, which retains as much of the customer's sense of autonomy as possible. And that, in turn, almost always increases the rate at which appointments turn into sales (assuming you have a great product and a reputable company).

Over the course of the entire sales process, the customer would have many similar mini-processes that had been optimized to increase engagement in this way and retain the customer's sense of autonomy, which resulted in significantly higher performance for the sales team.

Customizing your own sales tool enables you to create optimized, interactive mini-processes throughout your presentation that can be accessed easily and quickly. That's really hard to achieve when you're using a bunch of disjointed, off-the-shelf sales tools, where designing a system from scratch with the customer's input might not be practical.

EMPOWERING REPS, PRESERVING AUTONOMY

Mike first began to design customized sales technology specifically because he wanted to enable middle-performing sales reps to present and respond during sales meetings with the same skill and responsiveness as the top performers. That was his goal, and that is ultimately what we achieved through the technology.

When he first started in sales, Mike found a lot of success by sticking with the script that he'd been given. However, occasionally he was confronted with a tough question that the current version of the script didn't handle well. In those instances, his physics and engineering background enabled him to answer where other reps might have floundered.

There was no trick to it. He just had the natural ability to answer hard questions off the cuff, which got many customers back into the process in a way that felt authentic to them. But that was just Mike's good luck. He had smart parents. He was a smart baby and had a lot of love as a child. He has a technical background, was a physics teacher in grad school, and he's very good at handling tough situations and unexpected challenges. Seriously, his gifts are many (note: Mike definitely did not write this paragraph).

Unfortunately, you can't expect to build a sales team with physics professors or naturally super gifted people (note: Mike needs to stop bragging). The pool of potential candidates would be too small. However, you *can* give other sales reps the same ability to handle tough questions and give high-quality answers when needed.

That's what Mike set out to do. To that end, he realized that carefully designed software could augment a middle-performing salesperson and their training, enabling them to get the same results as top performers without resorting to pushy close tactics. Now, instead of relying on non-repeatable charisma or other hard-to-replicate sales techniques, the results come from providing experiences like the one we described above. The end result is more sales, faster growth, and happier customers.

With customized software, customers get the feeling that the sales rep has full and complete mastery of product information. Tough questions don't trip them up. They can address more variables and handle challenges on the fly with ease. It really does change the tenor of the entire sales meeting, and quite frankly, it is the most efficient way to scale this kind of consultative sales with both a high one-call close rate AND high customer satisfaction approach that we've ever seen.

Some sales reps have a naturally exuberant, talkative personality combined with a sharp mind, and they are able to use both of these things to incredible effect. However, a customized sales tool can approximate these same gifts in just about any sales rep.

When Mike first introduced the concept of tailor-made software to Sunpro sales teams, he encountered a lot of skepticism, but the difference it made right out of the gate was remarkable. Our reps now had a resource at their fingertips during sales meetings that could keep them on script and enable them to respond to customer concerns on the fly. They started hitting quotas faster, and performance rates were boosted across the board. In the first territory where we launched Sunlighten (the application built for Sunpro), the conversion rate increased by 37% within the first month.

IS CUSTOM TECH FEASIBLE?

Maybe you've never considered the possibility of designing your own customized sales tool, but it's actually pretty straightforward if you have the right knowledge and mindset.

But first, you need to determine if it's feasible for your company to develop customized sales software. You want to create software that supercharges your sales game, helps your reps handle more variables, tackle all sorts of objections, and deal with tricky situations like a pro, not to mention the many benefits to downstream departments like operations, customer service, and compliance. Quite frankly, everyone benefits from having customized software like this, but here's the hitch: the payback period (or fixed costs).

Imagine investing a million dollars to develop software that reduces your median Time-to-Quota from nine months to 1.5 months. We've seen many teams achieve results like this after implementing tech and training rollouts of customized sales software. But you have to do the math to ensure the investment works for you. If the software costs a million dollars, will that reduced Time-to-Quote give you ROI? If you only hire four sales reps in the next twelve months, and they bring in a total of $2 million in sales at 10 percent profit margins, is that $200,000 of additional profit worth the $1 million it cost you to get it?

Maybe not.

However, once you hit a certain size, we'd argue that there's no better investment for a business than building this kind of software. You can expect quicker time-to-quota, better conversion rates, happier customers (due to greater autonomy and optimized sales presentations), and higher retention with sales reps. Do it right, and it'll be so game-changing that there's probably nothing else that should be a higher priority.

For us, it's crystal clear, black and white. We've lived through it multiple times, but if you haven't experienced it, you might not even realize it's a secret weapon in your toolkit. But here's the thing: We don't want it to be a secret! We think every large consultative sales team should be leveraging customized sales tech so no customer ever again has to listen to a miserable, pushy sales interaction.

The magic of this software kicks in within just a couple days of training. It's like giving a rep a turbo boost and freeing up more time to focus on nailing objections, perfecting scripts, and honing real sales skills. The result? Reps closing deals like champs, customers ecstatic with seamless info delivery, and fewer post-sale hiccups because the rep was in the zone during the sale.

Customized software is a game-changer, no doubt. With just a bit of script training, a new rep can be as good as someone who's been at it for years. That might sound too good to be true, but once you dive in and work with the software, you'll see the incredible performance. Heck, we've seen it enough times to write a whole book about it.

Remember, this powerful combination of a good sales script with customized sales enablement software was responsible for a tremendous amount of revenue in our business. We sold that company for almost a billion dollars. By that time, Gregg's team had grown from 350 sales reps to over 1,000, and all of that growth was entirely funded by our own profits. We didn't have to raise a bunch of money. It was our sales process and our software that made it happen.

The single biggest contributor to our tremendous growth was our ability to take people off the street and train them up in days, rather than months. And with the power of the software, they could go out in the field and perform decently right away. Turnover in sales reps tends to be high, so even a non-growing team tends to have a lot of new people to train every year. Even if your team isn't growing bigger, you will still get a huge benefit from getting them to quota faster.

So, are you ready to believe that software can be the unexpected hero in your business journey?

Before we go any further, let's be clear: You don't *need* technology to sell well. However, a customized sales enablement tool makes it *significantly* easier, especially for new reps, to walk customers through a purchasing decision. We can't say this strongly enough: If you haven't looked into using your own customized sales enablement tool, you are missing out on an unparalleled resource for empowering your team. Do yourself a favor and take a closer look.

IT STARTS WITH A GOAL

How do you even begin to develop your own customized sales tool? Good question. First, you need to determine what business objectives you hope it will help you achieve. Do you want to grow fast? Do you want to get new reps proficient in days rather than weeks or months? Are you trying to increase your conversion rate? Remember, you can set *higher* goals with good sales enablement tech, so don't be afraid to get ambitious! And be *very specific*.

What do we mean by higher goals? Examples:

- Increase the number of referrals per customer by 25 percent within sixty days

- Reduce the sales cycles from 60 days to 45 days in four months

- Increase customer satisfaction from an NPS of 7 to 8 within sixty days

- Reduce change orders from 20 percent of sold deals to 15 percent of sold deals within six months

Your goals set everything in motion, and they will be used to set up the customized sales tech. Once you have your goals, then you have to figure out how to create a tool that will help your sales team deliver your message. Remember, the primary purpose of a sales tool is to make it easier for reps to do a good job of delivering the script and addressing objections—especially those difficult objections that are tricky to deal with. And again, you get better and more effective scripts and processes with good sales enablement tech.

Once you've determined your goals, and you feel there might be a worthwhile return on investment for the software, then you have to decide if you want to use off-the-shelf or custom software. If you are a smaller company with a small team of reps, we would strongly recommend using an off-the-shelf product. If you're a little bigger, you might use software to integrate a variety of off-the-shelf tools. In either case, developing customized sales tools won't be worth the cost.

However, as the size of your business and total annual sales increases, you will eventually reach a point where it is absolutely worth the investment to create your own customized tool. It can seem scary to do this, but there's a fairly straightforward process to get your design in motion.

But you're going to have to put together a software development team and set some expectations around ongoing costs. That may sound like a daunting prospect, but we'll guide you through the process. It all starts with finding a good product manager.

CHAPTER FIVE

FIND A PRODUCT MANAGER

Every football team needs a good quarterback. Similarly, a software development team needs a good product manager. This is the individual who is going to guide your team. They do much more than simply bridging the gap between the business and technical sides of software development. They also become a business leader, sharing in the responsibilities of making strategic and tactical decisions for the business. As such, they are held accountable for their decisions and for delivering value.

Your product manager is going to work with you to find and hire developers, decide what features you want to implement in your sales enablement software, and, along with the engineers, be responsible for the building of a minimum viable product (MVP).

A good PM constantly reminds stakeholders (yourself included) to talk about problems, not solutions, because the solution design belongs to the PM and the engineering team. For example, you might approach the PM and say, "There's a concept that our reps are having trouble talking to customers about, and I can't figure out a good way to train people so that all the reps, not just the top performers, can address it smoothly." It's then up to the PM to find solutions for addressing this.

Finding a good product manager can be tricky, but we have some advice based on our own experience. First, you have to figure out *where* to find a good product manager.

So, how do you find this magical unicorn product manager?

Ask around. If you don't have experience in product management yourself, you're not going to have the skills to determine if someone will be good or bad at this job. Find out if people in your recruiting department have experience hiring product managers. Find a company that has a badass sales tool (as evidenced by references at that company exuberantly calling out their tech as the reason for their outlier success in a competitive market) and ask them how they wound up with it. Get references for product managers and then reach out to good candidates. Just be aware that a product manager who comes from a big existing software platform like Salesforce, Zoho, or Oracle, while incredibly talented, might also have some bias against certain kinds of outside-the-box solutions due to their past experience.

When you meet with a good candidate, ask questions about their past experience:

- Can you provide references of Sellers and Sales Managers and Senior Leadership where the product you created was the standout reason for their ability to win in a market?

- Have you built sales enablement tools before?

- What were the results?

- Did conversion rates go up? Over what period of time?

- Did the product facilitate better interactions between sales reps and customers? When it was released, how long did it take to make an impact?

- Were you able to create sales experiences where the sales reps didn't have to bounce between different applications and presentation collateral?

Ask anything you can think of that will give you a sense of whether the product manager understands what is required to really help a rep when they're sitting with a customer. And we're not just talking about making it easier to sign contracts or fill out forms. Do they understand how to make it easier to have an *actual conversation* with a customer?

At Sunpro, it eventually became prudent to hire a product manager to take over for Mike. Sunpro was in talks to buy Mike's company, and he was already involved in several areas of Sunpro beyond just the sales enablement application. We found an outstanding product manager named Chase Holroyd, who would later earn the nickname "freight train." How we found Chase is a good example of leveraging strategic connections. We tapped into our contacts at one of Sunpro's technology vendors—a vendor that would benefit from Sunpro's continued growth and had some insight into Sunpro's culture and expansion plans. It was through this vendor that Mike was introduced to Chase.

Mike had Chase spend his entire first month working as a sales rep with no product manager duties. This experience served several key purposes: 1) it exposed Chase to the current issues faced by the sales team, 2) gave him time to develop fresh ideas for support, and 3) allowed him to build strong connections with his cohort of sales reps and the managers involved in the training and his initial territory.

When Mike first suggested to Marc that feature development would accelerate if Sunpro hired a full-time product manager, Marc was skeptical. But within a few months of Chase starting, it became an ongoing joke about how much better Chase was than the "old" product manager!

Mike nicknamed Chase "freight train" because of his reliability and refusal to cut corners, even when under pressure. This reminded Mike of a train that has to stop at every station, even if it would prefer a direct route from point A to B.

TRAINING YOUR PRODUCT MANAGER

Once you've hired a product manager, it's a good idea to put them through your sales training, just like you would a new rep. They don't have to go out and sell, but they should experience the training first hand. Then again, if they *can* go out and sell, all the better! It may be terrifying, but it will be better for your business in the long run if they do actually sell.

Hey, we're not sadists; we just know how valuable sitting in the hot seat can be for people developing sales products. It's what made Mike so good at developing sales tech when he started (well, that and his natural cyborg charm and sunny disposition).

If your sales training is two months long, have your new product manager do it all. That means learning how to go on ridealongs, sell, present your product—the whole nine yards! (By the way, once you have good tech in place, training a rep should *not* take more than a couple of weeks to get them to the point where they are able to lead at least *some* sales calls.)

You can pay the PM a straight salary rather than commission, of course, but have them accompany your sales managers and learn to present as if they were a rep. Then your managers can determine whether the PM is able to take feedback in the same way you'd expect of a salesperson. Are they able to improve in areas where they stumbled? Can they catch their own mistakes?

This way you'll get a product manager with the skills of product management who also has a feel for your sales process from the inside out. Their job as the PM is to guide the development of your customized sales enablement software, so they have to juggle a lot of different responsibilities. They'll be working cross-functionally, identifying other roles that need to be filled, particularly on the technical side, and they will serve as a liaison between various teams in your company.

They're also going to take in a whole lot of business ideas, rank them, and turn them into the collateral that's necessary for their engineers to build from. Clearly, they're going to play a pivotal role throughout development, and you don't want them to try to learn everything on the job. They should already know how to guide a software development product from beginning to end.

It's not your job to teach them how to juggle all the different responsibilities of product management. They should already know what an agile methodology is, how to run the meetings, and how to create user experiences and stories from what you've shown them. And once they've been through your training and along for the ride (pun intended), they'll also know what they're trying to optimize.

CHOOSE WISELY

The product manager is vital to the success of the end product, so make your selection wisely. The product manager must be *very* influential with the person responsible for sales, so if the senior VP of sales doesn't listen to or agree with most of what the PM suggests, or they're not in the right mindset, then you don't have the right product manager.

This is why we encourage getting recommendations, not simply hiring someone based on their LinkedIn profile. Talk to other people in your industry (or related industries) that you trust and find good candidates based on proven track records of creating customized software. If you need to interview thirty people to find the right one, so be it. This one person will deliver so much value to your organization if you make the right choice (or deliver yet another clunky, annoying product for reps, if you make the wrong one), that it's worth the effort to get it right.

When you hire your PM, teach them your sales process. From there, they should be able to bring together all of the disparate teams and get them working together to decide what features need to be implemented in order to create a sales enablement tool that will optimize the customer experience at every step of the sales process.

In *The Hard Thing about Hard Things*, Ben Horowitz, an experienced product manager turned CEO and co-founder (now a general partner at the VC firm Andreessen Horowitz), describes an early document he created called "Good Product Manager / Bad Product Manager." He used it during his time at Netscape to clarify what a good product manager should do. Below is a similar approach, adapted for a product manager of a strategic, mission-critical sales enablement application.

A good product manager owns outcomes, even if they need to motivate people who don't report to them. They understand their product is mission-critical, a strategic tool with the potential to be the company's strongest asset. Titles don't matter to a good product manager. They communicate with senior leaders in sales, marketing, operations, finance, and customer service, doing whatever it takes to be heard. They speak the language of each business area and know the sales call methods as well as the best reps. They're accountable for ensuring the salesforce is properly trained on all significant new features. Good product managers know they're not just a cog in the machine; they drive the entire organization forward.

In contrast, a bad product manager focuses on activities, not outcomes. They might say, "I launched the feature, gathered input from those who showed up to meetings, and did my best. It's not my fault if people don't use what we built." A bad product manager misses critical opportunities and ends up managing a suboptimal product with clunky integrations, delivering yet another non-differentiating experience to the sales team and the organization. They don't secure buy-in from key executives like the CRO, CEO, CFO, or COO, so they lack support for their initiatives. A bad product manager talks to business leaders about features, scrum ceremonies, and technical integrations, complaining that they can't get traction or attendance in meetings. They can't debate with sales reps about different scripts and objection-handling techniques, and they delegate all training on critical new features to others. While they may run perfect scrum meetings, maintain excellent Jira records, and provide thorough reports, they always have an excuse for why they didn't make an impact.

The difference between a good and bad product manager often lies in knowing when to apply Responsible, Accountable, Consulted, and Informed (RACI) principles from IT Project Management. The best IT Project Managers ensure non-technical stakeholders don't create excessive risk. They force business leaders to either deploy necessary resources or admit that an initiative isn't a priority. A good IT Project Manager is brave enough to declare a project's likely failure and advocate for its termination if it's not viable. Similarly, a good product manager will say, "I don't see how we'll achieve this goal, so I'm reallocating resources to something we can succeed at." Organizations need product managers who can make these tough calls.

If a sales leader believes in a goal but can't achieve it personally, they're responsible for finding a way to deliver it—or stepping down. A product manager for a vital product, like the one discussed in this book, has a similar duty.

THE SPECIAL RELATIONSHIP BETWEEN HEAD OF SALES AND THE PRODUCT MANAGER

There may often be a gap between what the Head of Sales thinks technology can do for their team and what it can truly achieve when leveraging the concepts in this book. For instance, when Mike first presented his vision to Marc for the sales team, Marc didn't fully grasp how powerful a tool Sunpro would become. Here are some examples of how sales leadership learned to set the right expectations for the product manager at Sunpro.

One key moment was the initial launch of the application. Chris Nazario, a hardworking and highly effective Sales Manager, led the launch territory. He was strict with his team but open to innovation. Chris and Mike worked closely to fine-tune the application, incorporating territory-specific nuances and last-minute ideas that came increasingly from Chris and his team as they saw the power of high-tech integration with the sales process. While Chris's team already knew how to use their existing tools well, within the first month, sales in his territory rose by 37%. In fact, Chris's own godfather, Richard Villa, one of his reps, went from struggling to become the top rep in his territory. From then on, Chris and his team became a valuable source of ideas for impactful features.

This success, along with the new understanding of how much technology should support reps during sales calls, led to the rapid deployment of the application across the organization.

This set a pattern for sales managers to escalate the most pressing issues. "I'm having trouble with reps switching to a new lender if the first is a credit decline." "How should reps discuss batteries in this market given unique utility rules?" "When my reps need to recommend a new roof before solar, they struggle with presenting it well." "Only my top reps are meeting referral quotas."

The Head of Sales now expected the product manager to address these challenges and drive meaningful results. She expected substantial value from any time she or her team spent with the product manager's team.

If you're a major player in your industry, you'll know you have the right relationship between the Head of Sales and the product manager when off-the-shelf sales applications for your industry start adopting features that your organization has already implemented!

CHAPTER SIX

PUTTING THE RIGHT TECH IN PLACE

It should be very clear to your product manager that your goal is to facilitate better rep-to-customer conversations. Since you're hiring based on your recruiting and interview process, you know they've come to you with a lot of experience and proven track record. Now it's time for the rubber to meet the road.

Remember, our approach to creating customized sales software is to break down the entire sales process into twenty or so mini-processes, and then find ways to make these mini-processes more engaging and interactive for the customer. Our intention is to create a sales experience that better preserves the customer's autonomy, because that's going to boost all sorts of sales metrics. However, that's not the *only* goal of a sales enablement tool. You're also trying to help reps do their jobs better, faster, and more efficiently at every step.

Your product manager needs to play a pivotal role in figuring out how to do this. Show them the tools you're currently using and ask them how you could make them better. Demonstrate how your reps interact with the current tools (e.g., "They have to jump around from here to there.") and what your conversion rates are. Where does the sales team struggle? Which customer questions are the hardest to answer? Which mini-processes seem to remove the customer's autonomy?

If your new product manager is good, they'll start coming up with all kinds of ideas for how to create better conversations with customers and improve your conversion rates. And if you have multiple tools in play, they may start by thinking up ways to integrate them in order to make your process less disjointed.

Ideally, your sales leadership should feel empowered to challenge the product manager. For example, Gregg would press the PM on the parts of the process that only the best reps do well. He would want to know how a sales tool could help more people to do it just as well.

PUSH FOR SIMPLE SOLUTIONS

Sales leadership should be tightly coupled with the product manager and meeting regularly, at least weekly, to bring the most challenging problems to the product manager: "Here are the things that are keeping sales down. This part of the presentation is hard to get through."

Within days or weeks, the product manager should be proactively giving sales leadership ideas on how to improve conversion rates, because they will have good relationships with the sales team, gather lots of intel from sales team members directly, know the businesses sales scripts inside and out, and have a good idea of what the competitive landscape is like. The product manager should communicate to sales leadership what the options are: what kind of features can be designed to get the reps over that hump, and how much it will cost.

One issue that leads to bloatware and overly complicated UIs is the software team giving up too quickly on optimizing the Sales Call (the interactions between seller and buyer). Product teams working comfortably in the office may be satisfied with solutions that require a few extra navigations and clicks, without fully considering the cumulative effects on the user experience. By consistently pushing the technical team to streamline, simplify, and consider the application and Sales Call as a whole, you can counter this tendency. With months and years of this diligence, you end up with an effective strategic tool, while other companies, lacking this discipline, end up with software that's far less helpful.

Challenge the product manager to come up with features that

make the sales process as simple as possible. If the PM comes up with a UI that requires the sales rep to push multiple buttons through the presentation, push back a little. Encourage the PM to come up with a way to achieve the same thing with a single press of a button. You want a sales tool that makes interactions between the rep and customer better and better over time.

For example, in the world of residential solar sales, customers occasionally need significant roof work in order to maintain its integrity for the installation of solar panels. This created complicating factors for our sales reps, because now they had to introduce a bunch of roofing contractors for the customer to choose from, as well an array of shingle options, insulation, roofing prices, and so on. The sales rep received a small commission for roofing sales, but the complications often threatened to derail the entire sales process, which made those relatively modest additional commissions seem not worth the effort.

We wanted to make that part of the sales process less complicated. Actually, in a perfect world, a sales rep could press one button and magically set up the entire roofing process, but there was no such button.

The process of going through and whittling down steps to optimize for conversion is called (wait for it) *conversion rate optimization*. What your product manager should be doing is human-to-human conversion rate optimization, looking at your

sales process to find all of the pitfalls and complications, figuring out where customers are getting lost or losing a sense of
autonomy, and then suggesting features to fix those parts of the
process.

A good product manager should already have a lot of skill
around metrics, so they should be able to measure how a potential feature will benefit your team. They should also report on
the efficacy of what they're doing over time.

Bear in mind, there's not always a one-to-one correlation with
how an individual software feature will impact sales. Sometimes
you release a feature at the same time that the environment
changes or a competitor gets introduced, and it becomes difficult to track the resulting benefit. After release, try to measure
the impact, but assume that not every feature is going to help.

DESIGNING YOUR MVP

When you're trying to decide how much your sales tool should
be able to do, it's best to start with an MVP. Get your sales leadership and product manager to come up with a ranked order of
ideas for implementation. Create a two-column spreadsheet. In
column one, jot down your feature ideas. In column two, give
each of them a score of one to five based on how impactful they
would be, with one being "meh" and five being a game-changer.

For a more detailed assessment, consider adding a column that assigns a numerical value to the level of effort required to design and implement each feature. For example, a "1" could represent a feature that's very easy to develop (e.g., a couple of days), while a "5" could indicate a feature requiring extensive effort (e.g., "It would take a year and require all hands on deck"). Your product manager can help determine where each idea falls on this effort scale.

After you have your two or three columns, you can sort them based on which ones will give you the most "bang for your buck." Then, take the highest ranked idea from the list and figure out the least you can do to test if it's going to be helpful. Expect your product manager to battle you on just how little they want to release, but you need to be somewhat cynical about what's going to work. It's easy to rattle off ideas that sound like they would be helpful when they turn out to be absolutely useless in your particular situation.

	Feature, Idea, or Initative	Impact	Effort	Note
1	Tap < 3 buttons to add new roof to the solar proposal	3	3	
2	Change application color scheme to match CMO's new brand idea	0	1	
3	Leverage gen AI during appointments for 30% increase in time-to-quota for new reps	4	4	Large impact because 300 new reps are going to be hired next year

Together, you and your PM can whittle down the features to the smallest possible subset. Just get something out to the users so you can get real feedback from them. That is the only viable way to find out if a tool is truly helpful.

We've been in situations where changes made by software designers completely bombed in the field, and sales reps came to us complaining, "What the hell is this? Why do I want this? The customer isn't going to care about this feature." If the PM tells you that you're going to love some shiny new add-on, make them prove that it will actually increase sales. Test it.

Be aware, sometimes a lazy sales manager will blame the tech tool for their own substandard performance. They'll say something like, "My sales wouldn't be so low if only our software did this one special thing." A tool can make average reps perform at a much higher level, and it can help new reps get up to speed much faster. But it won't make up for reps or managers who refuse to do their job. The sales team and customized sales tech must be in sync and complementing each other.

Launching the initial MVP requires both strong product management and IT project management skills. In fact, launching any major feature after the MVP also generally involves IT project management. Much of the product's potential as a strategic tool for the organization depends on the product manager's ability to coordinate all stakeholders and balance their competing interests. The product manager must ensure that all affected departments are prepared to handle the additional workload that comes with something "new."

If the MVP impacts the customer contract, is the "contract review" team ready for extra work and unexpected issues? If it integrates with an ERP system, are ERP administrators prepared to make quick adjustments? Is Customer Service ready to assist customers affected by the MVP in case any critical process gets disrupted? Things will inevitably go wrong, so affected teams need additional capacity to manage these challenges quickly and maintain a positive approach.

Careful planning is essential to ensure that all affected teams are ready for change. This preparation should occur at MVP launch and with each major feature or integration release.

There were two pivotal moments for the sales enablement application: 1) the MVP launch (a make-or-break scenario) and 2) the first major integration between the sales enablement application and Sunpro's delicate instance of Salesforce, which functioned as an ERP system. To meet Success Criteria for both, Mike involved the lead engineer, Ronald Adonyo, in key meetings with stakeholders and sponsors. Ronald's rapid troubleshooting skills and his ability to quickly grasp complex issues made him an invaluable asset. Though not the most outgoing person, Ronald's brilliance and dependability were qualities Mike leveraged strategically.

In the first scenario, the key point person at Sunpro was Wayne Juneau, a veteran sales manager with a straightforward, no-nonsense approach. Wayne wasn't especially tech-savvy, but Mike saw an opportunity to build trust by involving him in collaborative meetings with Ronald. When problems arose, Wayne was quick to advocate for the team, using his strong communication style to protect them and ensure fixes and features were delivered promptly.

The second scenario was the team's first significant interaction with departments outside of sales. For months, Mike had heard complaints about the challenges of integrating external vendor solutions with Sunpro's patchworked Salesforce system. While vendors often promised out-of-the-box Salesforce integration, they'd inevitably hit roadblocks with Sunpro's customized setup. Integrating the sales enablement application into this fragile ERP system was a complex project that could serve as a case study in project management. One of Mike's tactics was to involve Ronald in working meetings with the system managers, where he acknowledged their hard work and collaborated on realistic, actionable solutions.

As key users, stakeholders, and sponsors witnessed Ronald's ability to deliver quick solutions, Mike knew that this buy-in would counter any backstage grumbling about the project. The trust built through these interactions would help defuse negativity that often undermines technical initiatives. Ronald's reputation became a protective asset for the project, keeping morale and support strong.

These dozen or so strategic (and admittedly costly) meetings spread across two critical initiatives over a year helped avoid countless hours typically spent on bureaucratic project documentation.

You should put effort into identifying and tactically leveraging experts for similar gains in organizational efficiency.

WHAT TECHNOLOGY CAN'T (AND CAN) DO

We've said this already, but it bears repeating: you don't need technology to do a good job in sales. It can help—probably far more than you realize. It will drastically reduce the amount of training needed to get reps selling well in the field, which will make a huge impact across the board on numerous sales metrics, but it's still not an absolute requirement.

Then again, fundamentally, you don't need cutting-edge technology to do most things. Humans built the pyramids without software, and NASA got to the moon with technology that would be considered rudimentary by today's standards. With good processes and good training, you *could* run a successful business on handwritten notes if you were organized enough.

If you wanted to use just a notebook and a pen, you could still sell, as long as you had a good process and script in place. But customized software is definitely going to make the sales experience a whole lot smoother and more scalable.

Before we introduced tech, it took more time and effort to get the same results. For example, way back in 2010, we used to have to climb up on the customer's roof to measure for their solar panels. Reps would scale a ladder and walk around taking measurements, sweating like crazy, and then come back down to the customer's living room to propose a system. And they didn't even know if the customer wanted the product yet!

Eventually, we heard about a then-new tool called Google Earth, and we started considering a faster, easier tool-assisted approach. We asked, "Could we take measurements to estimate how many panels fit on a customer's roof without physically sending a salesperson into a high-wire act?" Once we implemented that one tool, it made a *huge* improvement to our process. For one thing, we no longer had to train reps on safe ways to climb up on the roof and physically measure the space.

Indeed, the equation always works this way: *the better the technology, the less training needed for the same desired outcome.*

INITIAL TRAINING PERIOD

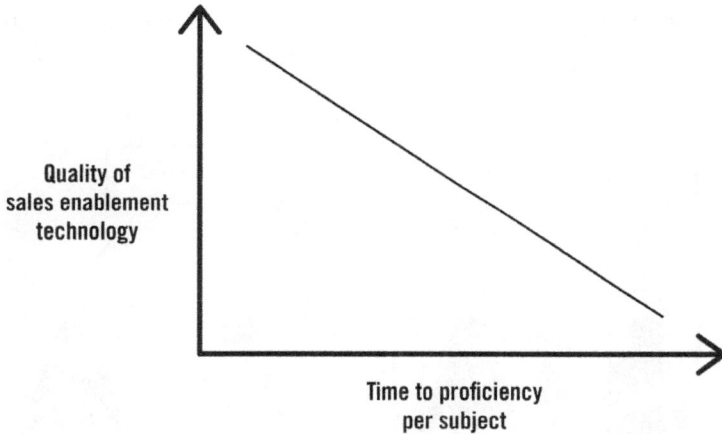

Quality of sales enablement technology (vertical axis)

Time to proficiency per subject (horizontal axis)

The right technology will almost certainly mean *less* training, but it will never mean *no* training. A sales process that would have taken multiple meetings to close without technology (unless resorting to high pressure close tactics), might only take one because you are optimizing the number of variables that sales reps can address in a single meeting, thereby accomplishing a one-call close AND still retaining high customer satisfaction. It can also help sales reps drive customers to a decision faster by facilitating the flow of the conversation and enabling the sales rep to perform at their maximum potential.

But your tool should be efficient, not distracting the customer with words or trying to take over for the sales rep. If the tool is designed to facilitate the Sales Call, then you don't want to put anything on the screen that distracts from what's happening in the room or does the customer a disservice. Remember, a sales tool is serving two users: the rep *and* the customer.

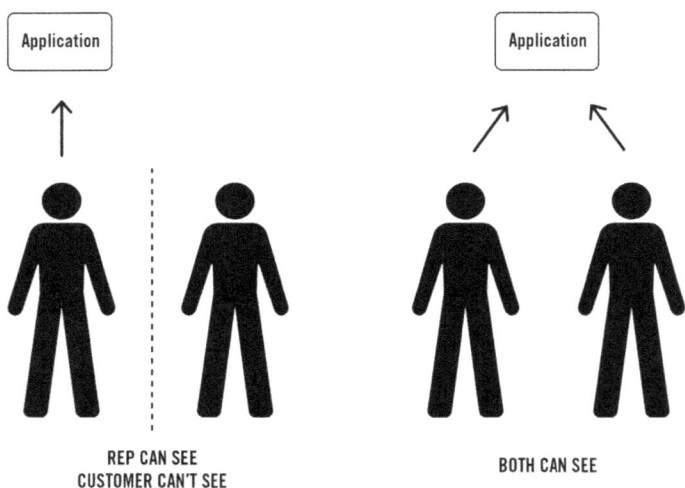

It should serve both of them well, making it easier to walk through the Sales Call and gain clarity. That, in turn, will make it easier for the customer to make a decision they can be happy with.

Ideally, your sales tool should increase the number of appointments that turn into sales by helping achieve clarity for all the topics and decisions in the Sales Call. If a feature doesn't do that, if a tool doesn't do that, then it's not serving its purpose.

Go to your list of ranked ideas. Conduct a cost/benefit analysis of each one and consider which ones are likely to actually help your sales reps and customers gain the clarity they need to make decisions. Don't invest in shiny toys that won't actually help create a better customer experience.

Always remember the two goals of customized sales software are to 1) optimize and address as many variables as you can during a sales meeting and 2) to do it in a way that preserves customer autonomy in the buying decision. If you do those two things well, then your software is going to make a tremendous impact on your outcomes.

While part of the reason we included this section is to highlight scenarios where actions may appear innovative but are actually shortcuts, here are specific areas where Sunpro was already excelling relative to competitors and took to the next level with technology:

1. Boosting Sales Rep Conversion Rates by 37% in 30 Days: Before Sunpro's core sales enablement application launched, the sales team had to use a PowerPoint, a thick brochure, a spreadsheet, an industry-specific CAD tool, various PDFs in DocuSign, a referral app, and a CRM system during a call. They were trained to use all these

tools, but consolidating them into a single tool for the sales call led to a 37% increase in conversions within a month. This improvement in a pilot territory with 10 reps was the proof Marc had been waiting for, and he quickly had Mike roll it out to the entire team.

2. Accelerating New Territory Profitability: One of the toughest achievements was Sunpro's ability to expand into new territories, hire reps, and reach profitability quickly. With an 85% reduction in new-rep-time-to-sale, Sunpro could launch a new territory, bring on new sales reps, and become profitable within four months.

3. Driving Referrals to 30% of Sales: Sunpro's internal team worked closely with sales managers and reps to create individual sales plans that leveraged referrals. Imagine a "referrals inside sales manager" encouraging a rep by saying, "Let's see how your numbers would improve if you got just one referral per customer." Sunpro's platform made it possible for even new reps to drive referrals, replicating the results of high-performing veterans who naturally receive referrals from existing customers. By building features to support this, Sunpro maintained 30% of sales from referrals, even while doubling the size of its sales team each year.

4. Increasing Roofing Sales by 200%: Sunpro installed solar

systems on residential roofs. When a customer had an old roof, reps faced the challenge of explaining options and answering questions about the timing, cost, financing, and how it would impact their solar installation. With the sales enablement app, Sunpro created a seamless experience, allowing reps to guide homeowners through the process, even if they needed a new roof. This resulted in the roofing division tripling its revenue within the first few weeks of the feature launch and significantly reduced cancellations for jobs requiring new roofs.

QUALITY ABOVE ALL ELSE

Making sure sales doesn't suck means creating a set of standards that you and your team can (and should) adhere to in perpetuity. That's the goal behind every manufacturing process and tool. You set standards and then use quality control and quality assurance to make sure you maintain them.

In the same way, you want to consistently deliver a high quality consultative sales experience to your customers, and you want a certain number of sales appointments to convert into sales each month. Those should be the standards of your company.

To get there, you're going to create a script, good training, and a customized tool to help every single sales rep adhere to the standards you set. Of course, you may need to develop different scripts and customer experiences for different locales. In fact, your sales "script" might actually be a bunch of different localized scripts. Even so, your standards should remain consistent.

Even if you are relentless about maintaining high standards, over time scripts (and therefore, sales tools) can become less and less effective because they were written to address a moment in time. As the world changes, if your script, training, and sales tools don't change, their utility will degrade.

In order for the sales reps to continue to do their job, they have to know when and how to change. They will need scripts, training, and a sales tool that keeps up with the times.

PART THREE

ROLLING IT OUT

CHAPTER SEVEN

PUTTING THE RIGHT
TRAINING IN PLACE

If you take the lessons from this book and create an effective consultative sales process, one that does a great job explaining to customers the problems your product solves and gives them enough information to make a decision they feel good about, then you might soon find yourself faced with a new problem: sales volume. Your new salespeople may start bringing big numbers in the door because of the stellar script they're working from.

But as your business grows, you have to make sure that your training rises to the same level as your fabulous new script. Great training ensures consistent quality presentations no matter how big your sales team gets.

But is this surprising? "You need training."

No, there's nothing novel in saying this, and there is plenty of great information out there about creating training curricula. General training advice is outside the scope of this book, so we won't spend time on the nuts and bolts. However, we want to share some of the things we've learned that need to be kept top of mind when you're developing your training program.

If you leverage sales technology well, you're going to significantly reduce the amount of time it takes for a sales rep to reach a high level of performance. Contrast this with traditional sales methods, which require extensive training on multiple tools and dealing with the limitations of off-the-shelf technology.

Assuming a fixed amount of time is allocated for training sales reps, this time is typically divided among various types of training. This may include training on HR matters, closing deals, script training, and product knowledge, but a significant portion of this time is usually spent learning how to navigate different sales tools.

However, if the technology is implemented well, it allows for a shift in the focus of training. Instead of spending all that time on learning multiple tools, more time can be allocated to high-quality sales training, such as practicing scripts, role-playing, handling objections, and dealing with unexpected situations that may arise—the kinds of training that will significantly enhance their performance.

However, there are two things in particular we want to touch on now that should be particularly helpful:

1. The importance of good sales managers

2. The best way to conduct ride-alongs

QUALITIES OF A GOOD SALES MANAGER

Okay, it's time for the first controversial statement of this chapter: Your sales manager does not need to be the top-performing salesperson in your company in order to be a good manager.

A sales manager is there to serve the team and help them get better at following the script, not to lord their past accomplishments over everyone. If they were great at their job, helped their colleagues, and prioritized values larger than just having the best sales quarter at all costs, then they will probably make a great sales manager.

High performing sales reps can be put into two categories, those that succeed by adhering to standards, and those that succeed but don't adhere to standards. It's the former that you want to consider for promotion to a sales manager.

So how else do you identify a good sales manager? Personally, we like to judge potential candidates by their fruit. Look at how the people around them are performing. Have they had a hand in the successes of other people, and do the people around them already look at them as a leader? A good sales manager can coach people well and likes to help other people develop more than they like listing their own accomplishments. As mentioned above, do they stick to the script and the process very well and use it to great effect, and do they model it for other sales reps? If so, that may be your person.

A sales manager should know the script better than all the other reps. They should be able to handle objections better than all the other reps, and they should be able to conduct ride-alongs and notice where a sales rep doesn't follow the script or handle an objection according to the standards.

You're not just hiring an administrator whose job is to get pricing sheets and provide product information. That's not nearly as helpful as your sales manager must be to your sales team. An effective sales manager helps their reps get better at the script in every way so they make more sales. In other words, they need to be really good coaches. Sales managers are what make a business go and grow.

It's the managers who have to be experts in the sales process as you scale your team, so pay careful attention to those sales reps on your team who:

1. Know the script backward and forward,

2. Are great at selling through the process,

3. Can handle objections well,

4. Make a positive impact and inspire other reps,

5. Genuinely care about the team, company, and customers,

6. And earn respect from other sales reps.

People with these qualities are more likely to make effective sales managers.

HIRE FROM WITHIN

Personally we believe it's a lot better to hire from within because they will already be familiar with your process. When you hire a sales manager from outside, you not only have to train them to manage the team, but you also have to familiarize them with your sales process at the same time. It is particularly important to promote reps who excel at following your process if you intend to scale your business, because your sales process is what makes it possible to scale and maintain quality.

But even if you promote a great sales rep who knows the process backward and forward, the transition to sales manager can be difficult. *Sales rep* and *sales manager* are very different jobs with very different goals. It's not always an easy change. Let's be honest, salespeople tend to be very extrinsically motivated! As the old joke goes, "Salespeople are coin-operated." In other words, if you want to change a salesperson's behavior, you change how they make money. Put money where you want them to focus, and they will follow it.

But managers must love to coach and develop people. They can't just chase the money or their own personal glory. That's another reason why you shouldn't automatically promote your top performer. Instead, look for salespeople who have a healthy balance of both extrinsic and intrinsic motivations. It's okay if they want a fancy car, big house, and lots of nice stuff, but if that's *all* they want, then they probably won't value training, coaching, and guiding other people as much as a good manager should.

KEEP THE PIPELINE OPEN

If you see good candidates for management on your existing sales team, start giving them opportunities to grow in those qualities that will make them effective sales managers. For example, give them team-oriented tasks, have them help new sales reps, and so on. Start preparing them for future leadership now, even if you're not going to promote them right away.

At the same time, you should be on the lookout for current sales managers who aren't making the cut. You should be able to ask any person at any time on the sales team to execute parts of the script. If they can't do it then that is a huge red flag. They need more training immediately. And if an underperforming manager isn't coachable or trainable, then they're not a good fit. A poor-performing manager or sales rep is almost certainly unhappy, and they are taking the place of someone who really wants that spot.

When you allow underperformers to take up space, you are cheating others from reaching their potential. Acknowledge that the underperformer would be a better fit somewhere else and let them go. Then reach into your pipeline and scoop out one of those great candidates and let them step into the gap.

By the way, don't put your sales manager in charge of too many people. An effective sales manager needs to be able to make time for ride-alongs, answering questions, and helping reps through the myriad of challenges they face, with enough time left over for administrative work and other things. This can add up to forty to fifty hours a week rather quickly. Sales tools, especially generative AI-based tools, are starting to increase the number of people a manager can handle, but at some point, even a good manager will start to lose the ability to properly focus on their team as more and more sales reps come to them with a variety of concerns.

One of the most important things a sales manager does are ride-alongs (real or virtual), because that's when they have the most (and best) opportunities to observe the script in action, to see where sales reps are dropping the ball, and to look for ways to refine and improve the process. We have some specific, actionable tips for conducting ride-alongs effectively.

ALONG FOR THE RIDE

On a ride-along, the sales manager accompanies a rep on a sales meeting or sales call, not to intrude or correct, but merely to listen and learn. Their primary goal is to make sure the sales rep has all the skills and tools they need to take customers through the script effectively and lead them to a buying decision they feel good about. They're also looking for opportunities to mentor, develop, and build confidence in their reps.

There is simply no better way to see the competency of your team than observing how they perform while in front of a customer. As we said, the sales manager is mostly there to listen and learn, but of course, if a sales rep is losing a perfectly good sale, the manager shouldn't just sit there silently and watch the boat sink. It's fine to jump in and start bailing water. However, if managers find themselves stepping in a lot, that's a problem.

So what should a ride-along look like?

Well, there are two kinds of ride-alongs. First, there are the kinds that happen during training, when a new sales rep accompanies a sales manager in order to discover how things happen in the field. Second, there are ongoing ride-alongs where sales managers accompany reps regularly for the sake of quality control.

We're going to focus on the second kind.

How often should a sales manager conduct ride-alongs in the field? We say if you are trying to grow fast, **at least twice a week.** That might feel like a lot, but the manager will learn things through ride-alongs that they can't learn any other way. They will discover what's going on in the market, and they can talk to their executive staff authoritatively about what's happening in the field.

If a single manager has twelve reps beneath them, and each rep conducts two calls per day, that's a total of twenty-four sales calls in a week. The manager should ride-along on two of those twenty-four calls.

Top-level reps may not need these as much because they've reached a level of proficiency where they clear their numbers, have a low cancellation rate, and know how to execute the process very well. Then again, we have learned a lot from going on ride-alongs with top-performing reps. For one thing, it helps you keep the script relevant and up-to-date as you learn new ways of walking through objections or explaining your products.

Most of your focus, however, should be on the middle salespeople. A sales manager should conduct one or two ride-alongs with these people every week, looking for coachability, teachability, and trainability. If they find that a particular rep isn't coachable or teachable then it's time for recruiting and replacing. The most time and resources should be poured into the reps who are hungriest to learn.

One of the biggest cancers in an otherwise successful sales team is allowing uncoachable sales reps to maintain their positions. Coachability speaks to character and is the foundation of a good sales rep. If a rep is *not* coachable, you probably need to move them on or you'll lose a lot of money from leads not closing.

If your processes have a proven track record of success, all sales reps need to do is follow them. An uncoachable rep often has excuses for not following the process—they feel it's too pushy, their opinions often conflict with the process, and they think they know better despite having no track record to prove it. Their paycheck usually reflects failure or mediocrity. They tend to bring other reps down, often gossiping. While they may agree with you in a coaching session, they revert to their old ways under pressure in a sales call. They lack discipline, letting emotions and feelings override the process.

Coachable reps, on the other hand, are the opposite. Spend time with them and help them succeed.

It's important to frame the "why" of the ride-along so the rep doesn't feel threatened by it or think they're doing something wrong. Often, a rep's nerves can lead to poor performance. As a manager, you want them to feel supported, knowing you're there to help. If they feel you're just taking notes and judging their performance, they may not perform well, and this won't accurately reflect how they work in the field.

You should conduct one ride-along with every sales rep during training so you can confirm that they know the process, and then go out with them again later to check on their progress. If there's a problem, then you need to get out in the field to find out what's happening. For example, if a new sales rep has had five appointments and failed to close any of them, a ride-along is the best way to touch base and find out how you can help.

When he was a sales manager, Gregg conducted three or four ride-alongs every week, focusing on new reps and the middle class. He only needed to touch base with his high-end reps when a new product was introduced. For example, when he hired Mike, he did a couple of ride-alongs during training and that was it. Mike started crushing it right out of the gate and never let up, so Gregg poured his energy into the mid-level performers instead.

You'll have to use some good judgment here. Are your high performers sticking to the process, or are they cowboys and cowgirls out in the field? Those cowboys might close deals, but they might also create a lot of problems post-sale, tend to over-promise, and have high cancellation rates. You may need to conduct ride-alongs with them to guide them back toward the process.

There's no need to be rigid about your frequency, but two ride-alongs a week is a good target to aim for. Create a schedule so you can rotate through your reps, then adjust according to your own judgment. Spend more time with reps in the middle or those who need more guidance. Ride-alongs present you with important teachable moments, so if you're struggling in a territory, they can help you turn things around.

The truth is, sales managers tend to get lazy. Gregg had a manager in a struggling territory who he incentivized to turn things around, but the guy just couldn't do it. He couldn't make any lasting change with his sales team. When Gregg looked into it, he discovered that the manager was holding seminars instead of going out into the field and guiding his team. He was all talk, no action.

But that's what lazy managers are like. They want to tell people what to do, but they don't want to be exposed. And going out in the field exposes weakness, not just with reps but with managers, too. It's not enough to tell people what to do. That doesn't change hearts and minds. You also have to show them!

When you have a territory that's struggling, make sure your managers are going out into the field regularly. Your regional manager may need to conduct a ride-along with your local manager to learn what the real problems are. A seminar doesn't cut it. Lots of talk won't fix it. Managers have to get out there and see what's going on.

TIPS FOR RIDE-ALONGS

Once ride-alongs are happening regularly, there are a couple of important things to remember.

1) JUST LISTEN

Sometimes, managers aren't sure how to help when they're out in the field. With script-based sales, the answer is simple: just listen. You're like a movie or play director sitting in a rehearsal room watching your actors go through their lines. The director might jump in if things go off the rails, helping the actors get back on track, but otherwise, they're just there to observe and verify what has been previously directed to happen, is in fact happening. What a director doesn't do is take over for an actor and act out their part for them.

Don't position yourself as the expert in the room. Rather, position yourself to the customer like this: "Hello, I'm the manager. I like to come onto the field to hear what our customers are saying and make sure our products are the right fit. The sales rep I'm with is the field expert." If you take over for the rep, they will never learn what you need them to learn. Hang back, offer guidance when necessary, but mostly listen.

2) POST-RIDE-ALONG DEBRIEF

A big question the ride-along is meant to answer is this: "Is the sales rep listening to the customer and applying their concerns to the script?" To find out, you need to be present and taking mental notes, or even better, be prepared to use an AI coaching app and ask to record. Note what they do well and what they could do better. Remember, the sales rep is going to feel nervous that you're there, so don't be too harsh.

After the ride-along, share what you observed, always starting with praise and encouragement. If you've coached them on some issue in a previous ride-along and they do better this time, make sure to emphasize the heck out of it. You can dig into the negative a bit, but speak as a coach and teacher: "I noticed that when you came to that decision point, you didn't pause and wait for the customer to answer. You kept talking. Why?"

The rep might answer, "I got nervous."

Then you can say, "Okay, but why were you nervous? What happened in your mind that made you not wait for the customer?" What you're actually doing is directly asking why the sales rep deviated from their training. That is an important pattern for you as the sales manager. Notice when your reps deviate from training, ask why, and let them know you expect them to adhere to the training. By asking *why,* you may learn something that will cause you to update the training at a later date. Value is added to your organization in either case.

During this coaching, be sure to treat the rep the same way you want them to treat your customers. Make sure they understand what you say before you move on. Show empathy, but provide actionable advice.

Now, if you're dealing with the same issue over and over with the same sales rep, then they might not be coachable, in which case, they might not be a good fit for your team. Time is a precious commodity: their time, your time, the customer's time. You can't afford to waste time out in the field with people who simply won't learn.

Sometimes, a rep thinks they know better than you, and they're convinced they have a better process. If that were the case, they would have the numbers to back it up. That doesn't mean you should never listen to them or allow them to contribute to a process change. But just like a sports team, a player has to demonstrate a certain level of proficiency before they earn the right to introduce new things.

One indicator of a sales rep with great potential is when they can identify their own weak spots. If you're on a ride-along, and the rep starts telling you where they fumbled before you can even get a word out, that's a good sign. That rep is hearing the coach in their own head and trying to learn from their mistakes on their own. Someone like that is usually destined for great things.

Early in his sales career, Mike made an unfortunate blunder while Gregg was present during a ride-along. It was a sales meeting with a couple, and Mike rather innocently asked them if they were married.

Mike's question touched on something unpleasant for this couple, and the woman got visibly offended and said, "What a thing to ask! Why would you ask us that?"

Gregg looked at Mike and, with a smile on his face, said, "Yeah, Mike, why would you ask that?" Then Gregg turned to the customers and said, "Mike is incredible at designing systems, but when it comes to sales, he's learning new things as well."

Mike apologized, recovered, and kept right on with the process from there. As soon as the sales meeting was over, Mike didn't wait for Gregg to point it out. He already knew he'd messed up, so he mentioned it and talked about how he needed to avoid similar questions in the future. To Gregg, this proved that he was coachable and had a lot of potential.

We're all going to make mistakes. All you can ask is that your team recognize their mistakes, try to learn, and not repeat them.

Ride-alongs give you the perfect opportunity to make sure every sales rep is constantly striving to get better at selling through the process, so make sure you are conducting them regularly. If the ride-along is being conducted in person, it's a good idea for the manager to ride there and back with the rep. That gives plenty of time for coaching on the way, and post-sale debriefing afterward. It also enables the manager to truly understand the rep's point of view, what they may be going through in life, and what they need. Lasting relationships are sometimes built during these ride-alongs, so don't undervalue them!

In fact, ride-alongs may be the single most important thing that a sales manager does. There is no real substitute if you want to know how things are going in the field.

CHAPTER EIGHT

WHEN THINGS NEED TO CHANGE

Your sales script is a living document that should adapt and evolve as your needs change, but those changes should be deliberate, well thought-out, and tested. The same goes for your heavily optimized sales enablement tech. If a sales manager makes the changes, they should use feedback from the sales team out in the field: What are reps learning? What are they hearing? Has the competition changed? What are the shifts happening in the political or economic climates?

If your team experiences an increased cancellation rate or decreased closings, that's an indication that you need to make a change. If you're missing revenue targets, it might be because your process is off. Constantly examine and question your consultative sales process, even if you think it's great, because if the world changes around you, your great process might start to produce diminishing returns.

When there's a problem, a lot of sales managers expect changes to their software to solve it because they are lazy. They'll say something like, "If we can make the software do this one thing, I promise our closing rate will go up!" It is very easy to ask for a change to the software. In fact, it is probably too easy. It requires great effort to make sure a piece of software doesn't turn into bloatware. Seasoned sales enablement technology experts know how to debate with sales leadership. High quality checks and balances need to be in place to determine which changes are actually beneficial, and be involved at every step of the software development cycle so that the very expensive process of developing tech has a strong ROI. Even with trustworthy technology leadership paired with great technology, it is still often worthwhile to go back to the basics when considering making technology changes for the sales team.

That means examining your sales process to figure out where customers are getting lost. Talk to your reps and see if they're making adjustments to the process out in the field. Take their suggestions and test them thoroughly.

FIGURE OUT WHAT'S HAPPENING

Industries are constantly changing. Products get better, people get better, and your competition gets better. And change starts out in the field. If you need to adjust your process, it will be reflected in the numbers and feedback from customers.

But there's a big question. Once you've identified that a change needs to happen, who is supposed to take responsibility for making it happen? And how?

One of the biggest mistakes companies make is allowing a disconnect to develop between the C-suite and what's happening in the field. Build reliable processes so the right information gets to the right people. Ensure that those processes feed into your sales process change mechanisms. Maintain an awareness in your leadership of what's really happening out there in the world with actual sales reps and customers.

There are key indicators that will tell you what's really going on. If a territory drops in closing ratio or cancellation rates climb, there's always a reason why. So make sure your sales managers continue going out into the field on a regular basis.

You have to do some real work to get to the heart of the problem. You might have to practice "the Five Whys," a process developed by Taiichi Ohno at Toyota (no, this didn't suddenly become a self-help book). The Five Whys is exactly what it sounds like. Someone comes to you with a problem, and you ask why, get their answer, and ask why again, until you've asked "why" five times in order to drill down to the root cause.

What does this look like in practice? In a sales environment, it might look something like this:

"Why is our closing ratio declining?"

Because customers are becoming more indecisive about buying our product.

"Why are they becoming more indecisive about buying our product?"

Because our product is no longer perceived as offering the same amount of value.

"Why is our product no longer perceived as offering the same amount of value?"

There are now competitors offering similar products, so customers are no longer convinced that our high price is justified.

"Why are customers no longer convinced that our high price is justified?"

Because we are not communicating enough value to justify that we cost more than our competitors.

"Why are we not communicating enough value to justify that we cost a little more than our competitors?"

Because when we created our sales script, we were unique in the marketplace.

Solution: Adjust the sales script so it communicates higher value against our competition to justify our higher prices.

This is a way to move beyond band aid fixes to solve problems where they originate.

THE CONSEQUENCES OF CHANGE

Remember, the reason you're creating a consultative sales process that is repeatable and scalable is to ensure that every sales rep delivers a consistent message and experience for customers. Your scripts and training create your standards.

Once you have documented standards, why not leverage the body of knowledge that already exists about how to make products and services adhere to standards? That body of knowledge is called "quality management," and it is composed of both "quality assurance" and "quality control."

However, the standards that work now might not work in six

months. The process that is helping you achieve your goals today might not help you achieve them next year, and if they no longer serve your purpose, then the standards need to change.

As the world evolves around you, competitors rise and fall, and market conditions change. Your sales process becomes the vehicle for making adjustments to keep your company moving toward its goals. Every single person on your team needs to understand this, and they need to expect changes from time to time.

How often should you change your process?

There's not a set frequency. However, if your sales managers are conducting those twice-weekly ride-alongs with sales reps, then you should have feedback coming in from the field at least twice a week per manager. As feedback comes in, gather it and present it at some agreed-upon interval (e.g., every two weeks), and discuss the implications and what it might mean in terms of process changes. If your sales managers see emerging patterns out in the field, then you need to sit down and discuss if a script change or sales enablement technology change (or both) should be considered to address a changing situation with customers or the market. (It may be that what should actually change is your product or service offering, such changes are outside the scope of this book.)

Stick with those twice-weekly ride-alongs, and you should pick up on needed adjustments fairly quickly, before a problem out in the field can really begin to fester. Just remember, when you make a change, you have to create a new version of your script and train reps on it. Once you implement the change, you need mechanisms in place to ensure that the new standards are being trained and implemented properly.

The last thing you want to do is introduce chaos into your sales process without actually moving your company closer to its goals. When considering a change, ask yourself the following questions:

- How many people will be affected by this change?

- How complicated will it be to implement?

- What is our process for integrating new processes into training?

- What is our process for ongoing training?

- What are the broader implications of the change?

- How do we ensure, once we make a change to our standards, that it will be adhered to in the field?

- How should our tech systems, especially sales enablement tech, change to support this?

Answering these questions will give you a fighting chance of being able to handle any problems that arise. Honestly, there will always be problems that you didn't anticipate, but if you do enough planning, the number of problems (and the severity of those problems) are more likely to be manageable.

Caution is advised, but again, you can't avoid change just because it's difficult. You don't want your team driving off a cliff because the road washed out in front of them. That's what you're doing if you resist making a necessary change to address evolving conditions.

Then again, there has to be a balance. If you try to make a change every time you perceive a change in the outside world, your team might struggle to keep up, especially if you're a larger company.

Small teams can change things all the time. If you only have a handful of people, you can make big changes and keep everyone in the loop easily. However, as your company gets bigger, the unintended consequences of a change may begin to outweigh the benefits. If you don't plan adequately for a change, it might end up delivering negative value.

The world of sales changes fast, and you need to be able to adapt, so you're going to feel tempted to make changes just as quickly. Slow down. Create a process for making changes that protects you from chaos by training your people well on understanding and implementing new standards. They need to understand the "why" of any change, or they might resist doing it.

COMMUNICATING AND IMPLEMENTING CHANGE

If you want to implement change effectively, you need to make sure your leaders are in agreement about what the objectives of that change are, and what success will look like. Quite frankly, if your leaders can't figure out how to define success, then you're going to find yourself in a pretty miserable situation.

You need a definition of success, and everyone connected to the change needs to understand your objectives. Give them a chance to provide feedback, but understand that ultimately everyone has to commit.

If you're working on an initiative that leaders across all departments recognize as important, then managing that project has a fighting chance of success. Mike's approach was, after ensuring the project's objectives were worth the time and treasure to the org, do whatever was necessary in sharing, socializing, and justifying an initiative so that the only way people could publicly disagree with its ongoing management was to be unreasonable.

We say this to help force the proper perspective, and to force the manager of the initiative (which could be the MVP launch discussed above, a major feature or a major integration) to think about things from the perspective of the stakeholders. This, by the way, is why it is critical to find product managers who also have expert Project Management stakeholder and customer expectation management skills.

For all the stakeholders you can easily imagine causing you headache over a change, ask yourself the following questions:

- Will this person think what I'm doing here is reasonable?

- If not, what should I do about that?

- Should I change what I plan on doing?

- Should I change what they *think* is happening?

- Should I create a situation where they will witness everybody else agreeing with the course of action?

- Should I make sure they see how much work goes into one aspect of the project, so they will stop asking for a million other things (or so they will stop disagreeing with me)?

If you have competent people working on scripts and working on your sales enablement tech, only taking actions that reflect your goals and make sense to all reasonable team members, then you're almost guaranteed a successful outcome in the long run. Just know that any change you implement is going to cause problems for some people, even if you do it right.

Reach out to those people, get them involved, and make sure everyone is aware of what's going on. Let people try and come up with a better option. Often, you'll all discover together that there *is* no better option, and the unintended difficulties are reasonable and necessary in order to adapt.

When you finally decide on a change you're going to implement:

- Make sure everyone understands what the project means and why you're doing it.

- Find the right person to be responsible for the project. Make them accountable, and make damn sure they believe in the project.

As the company grows, the negative consequences of projects driven by good intentions and a "just get it done" attitude will become more significant. The quality of your product and project management needs to improve accordingly. Otherwise, the features, initiatives, and integrations you implement may end up causing more harm than good.

TIPS FOR GETTING BUY-IN

Part of getting buy-in for a change is learning to communicate change effectively. This becomes trickier in a larger company or with a complex change, so let's look at some practical ways to get people on the same page.

If you're trying to get a high-profile project off the ground, especially one that might cause some resentment, and you need to get a lot of people in the know, first get approval from the right leaders. Then create a project charter, a document that outlines all of the moving parts, and make everyone read it during the first few minutes of a meeting. Here are specific tactics you can employ to hold accountability:

- Having people review the weekly update document at the start of each meeting

- Documenting opportunities for disagreement

- Tracking attendance

- Supporting the sponsor if they couldn't attend regularly

- Clarifying initiative roles

- Continuously asking for better ideas

- Regularly seeking confirmation that we've agreed on the path forward

- Noting when we've passed a deadline for suggesting alternative approaches

These practices help keep the initiative on track and minimize unnecessary conflict.

If you make a mistake with a project, use it as an example for how mistakes should be handled. Have the project manager or the responsible person own the mistake and call it out to everyone: "Hey, team, this is the mistake I made, and these are what I believe are the implications for everyone else. But here's what we're going to do about it."

Mistakes are going to happen, but if you use yourself as the example, you'll start to make a use case for accomplishing goals even in the face of errors. When you provide a framework for acknowledging and remedying mistakes, other people on your team will be more likely to tell you when they've made their own. By the way, the earlier you find out about a problem, the cheaper it is to solve.

In order for this tactic to work without creating resentment, you have to treat people well, keep things positive, and explain the value of what you're doing.

Another tactic for minimizing the chances of a poor outcome for a long-term initiative is to use *leading indicators of success* for your team. For example, let's suppose you say, "The purpose of this project is to generate more sales, but since it takes us an average of six months to make a sale, we won't know if this project made an impact for at least six months from when it's finished."

Sales is a *lagging* indicator of success. As time progresses, the reality of a lagging indicator will put more and more pressure on the team, so you probably want to look for *leading* indicators of success. You should be able to say to stakeholders something like, "Since we can't know if the project is a success until six months after the project finishes, we've figured out two other things that we can measure sooner that we think correlate well with our objective."

Here is an example that weaves together leading indicators and humor as an engagement tactic. At Sunpro, the product Mike had built was being integrated with their ERP system. Sunpro had previously attempted to migrate from an in-house Sales-force ERP setup to a NetSuite-based system—but that project had failed, and only part of it was ever completed. That project had an influential subject matter expert named Noel who was at that point skeptical of IT projects (understandably so). She also hadn't seen Mike manage an IT project. Mike used Noel as a team engagement tactic, and he got everybody on board with calling a specific leading indicator, "Noel's Numbers." At meetings, he would say things like, "Noel's numbers say we're going in the right direction! Isn't that awesome?" It was a specifically campy and humorous engagement tactic that worked with that team of individual contributors, subject matter experts and stakeholders.

In IT projects, the details really do matter. You, as the project or technology leader, or you as an exec accountable for a change along the lines of this book, must ensure that the right people pay enough attention to get the details right. People pay more attention, and feel better about doing it, when the leader gets these team engagement tactics right.

Finally, before you decide to implement a change, you can create a one-page document that outlines all of the systems and processes in your sales department, such as:

- Systems that come up with scripts

- Systems that come up with training

- Systems that deal with technology

- Systems for training new reps

- Systems for training managers

Write down what they are and how they might change in the future, including how often they might change. Share this with everyone you can think of and get their feedback. This document might change as you go along, but it will give everyone an understanding of what potential projects could be on the horizon. Create a first draft, make sure everyone is aware of it, and socialize it.

GET IN THE FIELD AND GIVE IT A SHOT

When it comes to new ideas for features and scripts, it's unfortunately all too easy to create ideas that seem feasible to too many people—especially those with power and influence. This phenomenon is so common it even has a name: the Dunning-Kruger effect.

To counter this, especially when it comes to scripts (the carefully crafted ways of communicating key points about your product or service), it's often best to find a trusted expert in your organization and have them "get in the field and give it a shot." On the other side of the coin, if an influential person is pushing for a particular script to be used in the field, and a knowledgeable subordinate believes the idea is likely flawed, it's wise to test it in the field on a small scale before any broad rollout.

This approach mirrors concepts from the MVP (Minimum Viable Product) creation process. Compared to the challenge of developing and maintaining truly useful scripts and technology features, listing ideas is the easy part. Dealing with this aspect requires constant diligence.

CHASING THE DRAGON

No matter how good your sales process, training, and tools are now, there's going to come a moment when good intentions and a get-stuff-done attitude aren't enough. Once you grow to a certain size, trying to keep a handle on everything is going to start to feel like holding a restless dragon by the tail. At that point, you'll have to make some big changes to stay on track.

Don't let it scare you.

If you're a sales leader, you don't need to know the process for changing sales enablement tools. That's why you have smart people like your product manager on your team to run the process. But you do have to be savvy enough to know how to rely on those people. Learn to trust one another. If you try to manage every change, you're going to burn out.

Remember, your job as a sales leader is to ensure that the right things happen and are well communicated. It's not your job to do them all.

CONCLUSION

We've recommended some big shifts in this book, and we're well aware that change can be difficult and complicated, whether you're a big or small organization. So before we go, we want to share a few examples of ways we've dealt with complications when implementing the things we've discussed.

If you're considering creating a brand new sales process, introducing a new customized sales enablement tool, or enacting some other big changes that will help your reps close more deals, our first and best advice is, of course, *do it*. As soon as you've defined the objectives, scope, and what success will look like, work on getting agreement from the people who matter most (those who can hire and fire). And once you have agreement, feel free to move forward on it!

If you're introducing something a bit more complicated, you may need to spend some time fleshing it out until you're able to generate proof that it will work. Put the terms of the project in writing ("We're going to need this much time, this many people, and this much money to accomplish it."), and get it signed by the person who has the authority to execute. Then use the principles we've outlined in the preceding chapters and do whatever is necessary so the only way someone can disagree with you is if they're being unreasonable.

Just remember, you need buy-in from all stakeholders, so be sure to communicate the value and benefits of whatever you're introducing clearly and compellingly. If you have agreement, then the people responsible for implementing it are more likely to be fully committed and accountable.

Be reasonable. Set expectations clearly with your sales team, from the ones who own the decision to those who manage the project. If you do this, it will help you avoid a lot of future complications.

WHEN REPS DON'T WANT TO CHANGE

Sometimes sales reps can be resistant to change, especially the ones who are already performing well. If a rep is already treating customers right and making a lot of sales, then introducing a change can cause a lot of friction. Don't allow your ego as a leader to mess with their ego, because they're going to win. If you get into a power struggle, they'll just go and work somewhere else. Really good sales reps can *always* go somewhere else to make money.

You're usually better off elevating reps who've experienced a lot of success by sticking rigidly to your process, because they can communicate its value to others. When you make a change, that person is going to stand before the team and say, "Hey, the sales manager showed me how to increase our closing ratios. I went out and tried the new script, and I closed two more sales this week as a result. Here's how I did it."

One example from a well-performing rep like this will do a lot more to get your team on board than a two-hour diatribe from a sales manager desperately trying to drill the change into the team. Get the rep to articulate how the change fits into your existing process and how it will help other reps succeed, and people will be swayed a lot more effectively. They'll think, "If it can work for that rep, then it can work for me." It feels achievable because it's coming from a decent rep, but not a superstar rep.

Do you see the difference? When the superstar sales rep talks about how to be successful, the middle class can't relate. They'll write off the advice as simply a product of that golden unicorn's magical selling powers, so they won't extrapolate it to their own process.

"Yeah, of course it works for *that* rep," they'll think, "but she's got Michael Jordan-level talent, and I'm the sales equivalent of a high school point guard. I can't expect to do what she does."

Instead, put someone up there who is not so polished. Let them drive the new practices. The successful but not superstar rep knows how important the process is. They will point their success back to the process the sales manager put in place, which makes the sales manager look like a rock star.

Then, when their customer satisfaction rate goes up, and they start out-performing the high-performers, even the unicorns are going to start asking questions. "Wait a minute. What are these reps doing? How are they getting such great results all of a sudden?" Soon, even those unicorns will feel compelled to start sticking to your script.

If so, that's great. Encourage them, bless them, train them up, and send them on their way. Then, after they've adopted it and are performing it to your standards, you can invite them to share their success stories with struggling reps. Word to the wise: have them write out those success stories and talk through the story with them. You want to make sure that what they say will help struggling reps know there is a path to success (i.e., just following the script).

Before every meeting where Gregg was going to bring out his top people, he would always have a pre-meeting to work out what everyone was going to say. He never just gave them access to 1,000 people without putting some fences in place. What comes out of their mouths in those meetings matters too much, so he always took the time to make sure they were on point and ready to play ball.

FINDING YOUR OWN REPLACEMENT

Now, one more bit of advice before we sign off. A good sales leader always holds their position with an open hand, and that means they're always trying to find their own replacement. A good sales leader is always going to have opportunities coming their way, so hold your position with an open hand and look for other people who you can elevate. When you're in meetings, help mentor those people, help them get better at their craft, and prepare them.

When your subordinates see that you're elevating them and letting them have a voice with the executive staff, they're going to work harder for you. They'll be driven to perform. They'll see that you're a humble leader who wants the best for them. Always be driving for their success.

Then, if the market shifts, or the company grows, and you need to split territories or grow into another region, you'll already know who your leaders are. You know who can perform, and who you can send off to plant the company flag somewhere new. If a change needs to be implemented, they can implement it. Being a leader who raises people around you is critical to a successful sales team.

Markets change, conditions change, and problems of various kinds are inevitable. Whatever comes your way, take it to your people, figure out what the goals are, build a project around it, and go after it with everything you've got.

EVERYTHING YOU NEED

Okay, let's sum this all up. What do you need in order to transform the vast group of middle performers on your sales team into highly effective reps who can start performing at a high level in record time, close sales far more consistently, and create much happier customers (whether they choose to buy or not)? First, you need a sales process that includes a compelling script: both a **Happy Path script** that tells a good story about the value you deliver to customers, optimizes the customer's sense of agency, and proactively deals with their **most common (or "primary") objections**, and additional scripts for dealing with **less common (or "secondary") objections.**

Second, you need an effective training program that treats your reps like actors who are learning how to deliver their lines powerfully again and again and again. Remember, training is not just a one-time deal. With every change, you need to make sure people understand what the change is and why it matters. Additionally, your sales managers need to spend time doing ride-alongs so they know how things are really going. A process can look good on paper and be a mess out in the field, so there's no substitute for ride-alongs.

Third, if you can afford the investment, we strongly recommend that you consider providing your team with a customized, all-in-one sales enablement tool that can augment behaviors to drive consistently optimized experiences and sales.

Finally, remember that nothing is set in stone. Any part of your process must be adaptable when conditions change, and you need to constantly examine what you're doing to make sure it still works for you.

Friends, it's really no more complicated than that. Create a good scripted process that tells a compelling story, train your people to *stick to the script,* get your sales managers out in the field, and give reps the tools they need to create a consistent, high quality sales experience. If you do that, you're going to see that great middle class of reps start crushing it with sales.

We've given you plenty of practical steps, tactics, and guidance for doing all of these things, but it's up to you to get the ball rolling.

Good luck, and happy selling!

ACKNOWLEDGMENTS

To everyone who contributed to Sunpro's success, we owe you a debt of gratitude. The journey was challenging, inspiring, and ultimately transformative, thanks to each of you. Your hard work, dedication, and expertise laid the foundation for everything we accomplished at Sunpro. We're honored to recognize you here:

Stacy Adams, Savanna Beals, Craig Berner, Shannon Brewer, Jerry Carpenter, Melissa Donnow, Norman Farr, Cindy Foxworth, Matt Graham, Darren Gomez, Jill Jones, Wayne Juneau Jr., Kara Juneau, Kim Marshall Seidel, Kristie Moser Cross, Chris Nazario, Vicente Nazario Jr., Mary Anne Polson, Dustin Posey, Shaan Rahi, Dean Scott, Chais Sweat, Ethan Stephens, Bryan Troegel, Trey Wheatley, Richard Villa, Kevin Villars, Rodney Boyd

Marc Jones– Sunpro's success, the insights within this book, and so much of what we achieved would not be possible without your vision. Your belief in us and passionate commitment to innovation allowed us to push beyond limits, shaping not only Sunpro's future but our own paths as well. Thank you for being a driving force behind our success.

FROM GREGG

I want to give my deepest thanks to my incredible wife, Laura, and my son, Sky, who had to deal with my constant pacing back and forth as I worked through sales scripts. And to my daughter, Piper—my main sounding board when she was just six years old. When I first tested my scripts with her, I thought, "If my six-year-old can understand this, then I've nailed it." Piper would give me that sideways, curious look when she didn't quite get it, but once she understood, she'd smile. I knew I had it once she said, "Dad, why doesn't everyone go solar?"

Thank you to Josh Powell, who took a chance on this "mainlander," and to Henk Rogers, the creator of Tetris, for your inspiration. And finally, thank you to God. WOW!

FROM MIKE

To my wife, Raisa—thank you for putting up with your "robotic" husband and for reminding me there's life beyond work. To my mom, who provided me with everything I needed to dream big and accomplish what I have. And to my dad—thank you for being the ultimate role model: honest, smart, and tirelessly hardworking.

I also owe a big thanks to our early team at Patter AI—Chase Holroyd, Ronald Adonyo, Randy Acres, Soek Yie Phan, and Taylor White. You guys took our oversized vision and helped turn it into something real. Together, we're building a platform that's changing the game for consultative sales, making our powerful tools and processes accessible at scale.

To everyone who has been a part of this journey, thank you. Our success was, and will always be, shared with each of you.

ABOUT THE AUTHORS

MIKE LATCH is an entrepreneur and executive driven by the belief that the right blend of technology and strategy can drive massive scale. With over 25 years of experience in electrical engineering, physics, and sales, Mike has tapped into the unique insights of how technology and process can revolutionize sales strategy. As CEO of Patter AI, he continues to champion these revolutionary tech-driven strategies that supercharge strategic sales and has been instrumental in the extraordinary growth of several high profile companies.

GREGG MURPHY is a sales leader and CRO with decades of experience in unlocking people's maximum potential. Throughout his 25+ year career in solar energy and strategic sales, Gregg has been instrumental in driving business growth and cultivating award-winning sales teams. His expertise lies in transforming strategic sales processes, recruitment strategies, and training programs to maximize team performance across various organizations. As a dedicated leader, he has guided sales teams to achieve remarkable results.

www.ingramcontent.com/pod-product-compliance
Lightning Source LLC
Chambersburg PA
CBHW031850200326
41597CB00012B/354